COLLEGE BOUND

PRACTICAL APPROACHES TO NAVIGATING
ROOMMATE CHALLENGES, MANAGING TIME,
AND BALANCING ACADEMIC & SOCIAL LIFE -
YOUR FIRST STEP TO COLLEGE SUCCESS

ROSE LYONS

CONTENTS

PAY IT FORWARD

A SHINING OPPORTUNITY TO HELP ANOTHER YOUNG ADULT LIKE YOU!

WANT TO HELP OTHERS?

Thanks for picking up "College Bound: Practical Approaches to Navigating Roommate Challenges, Managing Time, and Balancing Academic & Social Life." As you dive into this guide, we're excited for it to become your secret weapon in conquering college life.

If a chapter really speaks to you or totally clicks, why not share the love? Your review could be the insider info that another student needs. Whenever you're ready, drop us your thoughts – they mean a lot to us and your fellow students.

Cheers to having you on board. Eager to hear how you rock your college journey with these strategies!

Brooklyn,

From the very start, when I first cradled you, it was pretty clear you weren't your average kid — tons of energy, always curious, and never afraid to dive into things headfirst! You were like a little tornado, and keeping up with you was an adventure in itself, but one I wouldn't trade for anything.

Now, you've grown into this incredibly kind, happy, and downright goofy daughter, and that boundless energy of yours is still just as infectious. Thanks for being authentically you and never being afraid to be yourself. I couldn't be prouder of the amazing adult you're turning into.

As you step into your next big chapter, remember one thing: I'm your biggest fan. You're going to rock this world, and I can't wait to see all the awesome stuff you'll do. Here's to you and your never-ending supply of energy! And just so you know, there's absolutely nothing you could ever do to change how much I love you.

With all my love and endless support,

Mom

INTRODUCTION

Picture this: you're on the edge of something big, like really big. Can you feel the winds of change ruffling your hair? Okay, maybe that's a bit cheesy, but here's the deal: college life is about to unfold before you. It's more than just heavy textbooks, huge lecture halls, and those midnight ramen sessions.Whether it matches what you've seen in movies or heard from your older sibling, college is going to hit you differently. It's a major turning point, like a real metamorphosis. Seriously, it's that deep.

You're leaving behind the familiar hallways of high school and the cozy vibes of your hometown for a completely new and exciting adventure. How cool is that? But here's the thing, you're not alone in this. Your excitement, fears, hopes, and jitters? Trust me, tons of people feel the same way.

Meet Anna, this valedictorian with dreams as bright as a supernova. She steps onto campus, all ambitious and ready to conquer the world. But guess what? She quickly realizes that this place is a battleground of talent and brains, and her confidence takes a hit. Sound familiar? It's that moment we all go through when faced with sky-high expectations.

Then there's Ben, our resident gaming enthusiast, looking to find some peace in the college chaos. But guess what again? College is nothing like the serene haven he imagined. It's more like a whirlwind. Ever felt like your dreams clashed with reality? Ben sure has.

And don't forget Carlos, bursting with hope and dreams of engineering glory. But guess what one more time? Life hits him with budget woes, tight schedules, and language barriers. Still, he keeps on trucking. We've all been there when life takes a detour from our perfectly planned routes.

Now, you might be thinking, "I don't know these folks." Well, no duh! But their stories might just hit close to home once you're settling into college. You might find pieces of your own journey in their struggles and triumphs. You may know them after all.

But hey, let's get one thing straight. This book isn't here to scare you with tales of insurmountable obstacles. Nope. It's all about embracing the ups and downs, growing up, and dancing to the rhythm of gaining wisdom together with your college community. You got this!

I'm Rose Lyons, here to be your trusted companion on this

exhilarating journey. Unlike many self-help authors who offer the same tired advice, I aim to be more than just a writer; I want to be your friend and mentor throughout this book.

As you embark on the electrifying adventure of your freshman year, consider this book your beacon of guidance. Think of it as your support system, ready to assist you in navigating the challenges that are bound to come your way. This isn't just a collection of pages; it's your road map through the uncharted territory of college life, a valuable resource to help you tackle the hurdles that lie ahead. And always remember, your victories are not a matter of 'if,' but 'when.' You've got the potential for greatness!

1 INTO THE UNKNOWN

The only true wisdom is in knowing you know nothing. –Socrates

You might be surprised that a staggering 64% of college students are leaving their college education (31 Alarming College Students, 2022). And here's the kicker – it's not because they can't handle the academic or financial aspects. Nope, the real challenge often lies in the emotional and mental toll that college can take. Let's take a closer look at this hidden issue that's affecting campuses everywhere, casting a shadow on the future dreams and aspirations of tomorrow's leaders.

Close your eyes for a moment and envision once-vibrant university hallways, once buzzing with energy, now resonating with the silent echoes of despair. Young, hopeful minds fresh out of high school step into these corridors with dreams as diverse and radiant as autumn leaves swaying outside. They see college as the golden ticket to a promising future. Little do they know, beneath this shimmering facade lies a landscape of emotional turbulence and mental burdens, turning the college experience into an intricate obstacle course that many find too challenging to navigate.

The unspoken, ever-present specter of academic rigor in college often preys on students' peace of mind. It's akin to an ongoing academic Olympics, where everyone is vying for success in their chosen fields. However, the real challenge often lies beyond the academic load – it's the concealed emotional strain that lurks in the background. This strain encompasses stress, fear of inadequacy, and the anxiety of unmet expectations. These mental adversaries can erode a student's resilience, sometimes more significantly than the academic challenges themselves.

To counteract this, mastering time management becomes crucial. Learning to effectively manage time not only aids in coping with academic demands but also in balancing social life. Effective time management techniques can help mitigate stress and bolster academic success.

In addition to academic pressures, many students grapple with isolation in college. Transitioning from familiar environments to new settings can be daunting and may lead to feelings of alienation, which exacerbates stress and anxiety. Learning to balance social interactions and forge meaningful connections can provide a buffer against this isolation.

Financial pressures compound these challenges. The burden of tuition, housing, and living expenses weighs heavily, leading many to juggle part-time work with their studies. This balancing act can be draining, both mentally and emotionally.

Unfortunately, many college campuses lack sufficient mental health resources to support students through these multifaceted challenges. This chapter seeks to illuminate these issues, exploring their manifestations, consequences, and strategies for overcoming them. It emphasizes the importance of developing skills in time management, social engagement, and personal care as essential tools for navigating the complex terrain of college life

The Truth Will Set You Up for Success

Undoubtedly, it's a breeze to get caught up in the wave of rumors and partial truths that create a somewhat skewed image of what college life holds in store. And it's not inaccurate to say that your college journey will likely encompass these quintessential aspects. However, it's also important to acknowledge that the real college scene comprises elements that may not conform to the typical stereotypes.

So, rest assured, you haven't been fed a pack of lies. But here's the scoop – there's more to the college experience than meets the eye.

Myth 1: College Equals Endless Parties

Truth: While movies like "Animal House" and "Revenge of the Nerds" may make it seem like college is one never-ending party, the reality is quite different. Yes, there are parties, and yes, they can be memorable, but they're just one part of the college experience. For every wild night out, countless nights are spent studying, preparing for exams, and working on assignments. The allure of a non-stop party life needs to be balanced with the sobering truth of academic responsibilities.

Myth 2: The "Perfect" College Ensures Success

Truth: The idea that attending an Ivy League or top-tier college guarantees a perfect life is a common misconception. Where you go to college influences your education but doesn't determine your success. Your achievements depend on the effort you put into your studies, the real-world experiences you gain, the skills you develop, and perhaps a little luck.

Myth 3: Your Chosen Major Dictates Your Career

Truth: Your choice of major doesn't lock you into a specific career path. Many professionals find success in fields unrelated to their major. While your major equips you with a particular skill set and knowledge, it doesn't confine you to a single career track. Flexibility and adaptability often play a significant role in career development.

Myth 4: College Days Are the Pinnacle of Your Life

Truth: College can be a memorable and formative period in your life, as reflected in pop culture. However, the notion that these years are the absolute best of your life may limit your outlook on the adventures that await post-university. Life comprises various stages, each offering its unique and exciting experiences. You've already graduated from many life phases, and college is just one of them.

Myth 5: Professors Are Indifferent to Their Students

Truth: Despite their busy schedules and numerous students to attend to, most professors are not emotionless or detached. They are not the academic version of Voldemort or dementors. In reality, many professors genuinely care about their students' success and are willing to offer assistance when needed. Building relationships with professors can be a valuable part of your college experience.

Myth 6: You Need to Have Your Entire Life Figured Out

Truth: It's okay not to have your entire life mapped out when you start college. Most students enter college with varying degrees of uncertainty about their future careers and life paths. College is a time to explore, discover new interests, and clarify your goals. You have the flexibility to change majors or career plans as you learn and grow.

Myth 7: Everyone Else Has It All Together

Truth: It may seem like everyone around you has their life perfectly organized, but appearances can be deceiving. Many college students face challenges, doubts, and uncertainties like you do. Don't be too hard on yourself if you don't have everything figured out; you're not alone in your journey.

Myth 8: College is Only About Academics

Truth: While academics are a significant part of college, it's not the whole story. College offers many opportunities beyond the classroom, such as extracurricular activities, internships, networking events, and personal growth experiences. These non-academic experiences can be just as valuable in shaping your future.

Myth 9: You Must Excel in Every Aspect of College Life

Truth: Striving for excellence is admirable, but it's essential to remember that you don't have to be perfect in every aspect of college life. It's okay to experience setbacks, make mistakes, and ask for help when needed. College is as much about personal growth as it is about achieving high grades.

Myth 10: You Should Compare Your College Experience to Others

Truth: Comparing your college journey to others' can lead to unnecessary stress and feelings of inadequacy. Each person's path is unique, and what works for someone else may not be right for you. Focus on your goals, interests, and progress, and don't worry too much about how your experience measures up to others.

Myth 11: College Professors Always Have the Answers

Truth: Contrary to the belief that professors possess an answer to every question, they, too, encounter uncertainty in their fields. College is a place of exploration and inquiry, and professors often engage in ongoing research and learning to stay current in their areas of expertise. It's okay to challenge their ideas and engage in academic discussions.

Myth 12: You Must Stick to a Strict Major-Related Career Path

Truth: While aligning your major with your interests is essential, don't feel confined to a single career trajectory directly related to your field of study. Many successful professionals switch careers or explore diverse opportunities unrelated to their major. College provides a chance to develop various skills that can be applied in multiple contexts.

Myth 13: Professors Only Care About Grades

Truth: While grades are a part of academic evaluation, many professors genuinely care about your learning and growth. They value your class engagement, discussion participation, and willingness to seek help. Building relationships with professors can lead to mentorship and valuable career guidance.

Myth 14: You Must Graduate in Four Years or Less

Truth: The idea that college must be completed in exactly four years is a misconception. Many students take longer to graduate for various reasons, such as pursuing internships, working part-time, or changing majors. What's important is that you make the most of your college experience and graduate at your own pace.

Myth 15: College is Strictly About Individual Achievement

Truth: While personal growth and academic achievement are essential aspects of college, collaboration and teamwork are equally valuable. College provides opportunities to collaborate on projects, join clubs, and engage in group activities. These experiences enhance your interpersonal skills and contribute to your personal and professional development.

Key Takeaways:

As you start your college journey, remember that myths and truths are like two sides of the same coin. Navigating through the misconceptions about college with a clear understanding of reality is crucial. While college is a time of excitement and self-discovery, it's not always the picture-perfect experience that myths may suggest.

Now that we've debunked some common myths, you're better equipped to face the next section, where we'll explore what college feels like at first. Brace yourself for a rollercoaster ride of emotions, new beginnings, and unexpected discoveries as you step into this transformative phase of your life.

What Does It Feel Like at First?

Introducing Davis, a young and spirited individual who was tangled in a web of emotions as he packed his bags for the grand adventure of university life. His heart raced with a mix of anxiety and anticipation, questioning what lay ahead. Could he handle the distance from home? What about his old friends? And what kind of friends would he make here? The uncertainty was scary, but it was also undeniably exciting.

With a heartfelt farewell to his family and the familiarity of home, he hit the road toward the unknown. Doubts occasionally tugged at his determination, but his car wheels kept turning, taking him closer to his future.

When he arrived at the university, it loomed before him, a place steeped in tradition yet brimming with innovation. Even the air felt different here, carrying a sense of new beginnings. Those online conversations with his roommates had built up certain expectations, but meeting them in person was a bit of a reality check. They were different but also newbies like him, all seeking their place in this unfamiliar environment. His dorm room, once so strange and foreign, made him yearn for the comforts of home.

But soon after, following an outing with his roommates, he started to feel the sparks of excitement and independence that helped thaw his homesickness. Even as his accent became the subject of friendly jokes, he laughed along. Each day brought more introductions and fresh faces, making the experience feel thrilling and surreal.

Yet, that initial thrill gradually gave way to fatigue as time passed. During his first week, the excitement was replaced by the grind of daily routines. He even fell prey to the infamous "freshers' flu." But amid the coughs and sneezes of his fellow students, he found solace.

Davis's early days in college blended his expectations and reality. Looking back, his initial worries seemed somewhat comical. He had indeed plunged into a river of unknowns, but instead of being overwhelmed, he learned to adapt. Davis was now a university student, ready to embrace the ebb and flow of the college experience.

What Is College Like?

Imagine this: your first day, surrounded by an awe-inspiring display of diversity. Think of it as a vibrant mosaic, a tapestry woven from countless unique tiles representing different cultures, backgrounds, beliefs, and personalities. Each tile has its own story to tell, and when woven together, it creates a beautiful pattern of shared experiences and diverse perspectives. This, my friend, is the essence of college.

One of your early challenges will be learning to live independently. Depending on your perspective, you might be excited about answering only to yourself. However, consider that living relatively untethered, away from the guidance of your guardians, is akin to surviving in the wild: you have the freedom to enjoy the beauty of nature, but you also need to build your own shelter. From handling laundry to managing your budget, you'll become a master of various life skills. You'll establish your own routines, learn to respect others, and even become adept at settling disputes over the last slice of pizza.

Many college nights will be serene, with only the rustling of leaves or the soft tapping of keyboards to disturb the quiet. These peaceful moments often open the door to introspection, where you'll contemplate your path, progress, or even the latest plot twist in your favorite TV series. In college, balance is key. You'll discover when to relish solitude and when to embrace the company of others.

Then there's the ever-present companion of college life: stress. It may rear its head during late-night study sessions racing against deadlines, or trying to juggle your social life. But within that stress, and sometimes because of it, you'll tap into the resilience of your spirit. You'll develop ingenious time-management skills, learn to prioritize, and, most importantly, mature enough to seek help when needed. This leads us to self-discovery. College offers you the time and space to chisel out your self-portrait, uncovering your passions, strengths, and limitations, and, in the process, getting to know yourself in ways you've never imagined.

The truth about college is that it's a dynamic, unscripted, and enriching journey. It's not merely a stepping stone to a degree; you'll experience a symphony of victories, challenges, laughter, and learning, all interwoven with a healthy dose of chaos. It's the space where you evolve from an eager freshman into a confident graduate armed with a sharp mind, a broader perspective, and a profound understanding of yourself. Welcome to the adventure.

Fail Proof Yourself

A small-town boy, Alex, sets off on his college adventure, a mix of excitement and nervousness swirling in his stomach. His hometown, where everyone knows everyone, and life ambles at a leisurely pace, feels worlds apart from the bustling university campus. In a dorm room shared with city-slicker roommates who seem to have life figured out, discussing concepts he's never heard of and jetting off to places he's never dreamed of visiting.

College classes hit him harder than anticipated. The whirl-wind of fast-paced lectures and intricate subjects leaves him grappling to keep up. The library becomes his haven, an escape from the constant feeling of being out of his depth. He tries to fit in, joining study groups in the hope of making friends and grasping his coursework better, but often finds himself overshadowed by his more outspoken peers.

Financial pressures exacerbate his stress. While his scholar-ship covers part of his tuition, the rest is a relentless source of anxiety. He takes on a part-time job at a local café, serving coffee to students who chatter animatedly about upcoming adventures and sought-after internships. Every shift is a stark reminder of the wider world he yearns to explore.

Navigating the social scene at college becomes an enigma he can't quite solve. Invitations to parties and gatherings come his way, but he often declines due to work commitments or the gnawing fear of not fitting in. When he does attend, he feels like a silent observer, watching others effortlessly navigate this unfamiliar terrain.

As weeks blend into months, the mounting pressure starts to weigh him down. He keeps up a facade for his parents over the phone, trying to sound upbeat, but they sense the underlying distress. One fateful night, after a particularly grueling exam, he reaches his breaking point. Doubt seizes him, questioning if college is truly his path and if he's built for this life. His thoughts turn to his family and the sacrifices they've made, wondering if he's letting them down.

Eventually, Alex makes the agonizing decision to leave college. Returning home, he carries a mix of relief and disappointment. His parents, though supportive, hold concerns about his future. Back in his hometown, he reconnects with old friends and lands a job at a local hardware store. It's here that he begins to realize the value of the skills he picked up in college—time management, resilience, and self-sufficiency —all of which prove immensely beneficial beyond the classroom.

Determined to continue his education, Alex opts for online courses, forging his own path at a pace that suits him. In this new chapter of life, he finds fulfillment in the delicate balance of work, study, and living in the comforting embrace of his familiar surroundings. However, as he delves deeper into his online studies, he begins to yearn for the vibrant atmosphere of a college campus.

Alex comes to realize that he wants to return to college, armed with newfound wisdom and a better understanding of himself. With a more balanced approach to life and a renewed sense of purpose, he feels mentally prepared to embrace the challenges and opportunities that await him on a college campus once more. This decision marks a pivotal moment in his journey, demonstrating the resilience of the human spirit and the capacity for growth and change.

Set Yourself Up for Success

Let's delve into the mental aspect, where college life can resemble a seesaw, swinging between exhilarating highs and unsettling lows. It's perfectly normal to feel overwhelmed at times, but what sets you apart is the strength of your mental state. Nurturing a growth mindset that welcomes challenges, embraces the effort required for mastery, learns from feedback, and draws inspiration from the successes of others can keep you afloat, even in the choppiest of waters.

Success in college transcends merely securing top grades. While your GPA is one measure of success, true education encompasses more. Graduating with emotional intelligence, nurturing symbiotic relationships, and expanding self-awareness are vital facets of your journey. This entails recognizing and effectively managing your emotions and using them to guide your thoughts and actions. As mentioned, college offers a delightful mix of diverse cultures, perspectives, and ideas, which can open your mind and draw wisdom from every corner.

Mastering time management is another key to your triumph. If you decide to immerse yourself in college life fully, you'll contend with lectures, assignments, exams, social events, and extracurricular activities. However, if you invest in time management skills, you can meet your academic responsibilities while carving out space for leisure and relaxation.

Many college students face challenges because they lack a robust support network. College can sometimes feel isolating, and if you're naturally introverted, you might find it challenging to connect with others. It's crucial to forge bonds with your peers, engage in clubs and events, and be unafraid to seek help.

However, the most critical strategy of all is developing a self-care routine. Your journey through academia may become arduous if you neglect healthy eating, adequate sleep, and necessary breaks. Prioritizing your mental well-being is equally essential. Consider incorporating exercise to reduce stress, elevate mood, and sharpen cognitive abilities. Explore yoga, meditation, or any activity that quiets your mind and enhances focus.

While it would be lovely if success in college could be achieved effortlessly, the reality is that it demands a specific set of skills. Mental resilience, emotional maturity, adaptability, effective time management, strong support systems, and self-care are all integral components. Remember that every challenge on your path is also an opportunity to grow stronger and wiser. Heroes are not forged by comfort and ease; your resilience in the face of adversity is what shapes your character.

The Good, the Bad, and the Ugly

Embracing Dawn: Zion's Morning Marvel

Zion's story at Evergreen University isn't just about classes; it's about finding a rhythm in the chaos of college life. He navigates late-night study sessions, roomie jamming, and lazy afternoons in the quad, where frisbees fly and laughter echoes. His weekends are a mosaic of dorm movie nights and exploring the city's hidden gems with Craig.

Aria's freshman year at Rookfield Institute is a vibrant journey of self-discovery outside the classroom. She dives into cultural festivals, exploring new cuisines with friends, and finds solace in quiet coffee shop corners, journaling her thoughts. The art club becomes her sanctuary, where she paints and connects with fellow artists, while spontaneous road trips and star-gazing nights fill her with a sense of wonder and belonging.

While the ultimate goal of your college journey is to attain that coveted degree or diploma, there's so much more to explore along the way. Let's dive into the strategies that can help you build a solid foundation for your academic success.

Key Takeaways

- **College Life Is Full of Surprises**: College freshmen should be prepared for the unexpected. Like Aria, embrace the unpredictability and find joy in the twists and turns of your journey.
- **Diverse Connections Enrich the Experience**: Embrace connecting with people from diverse backgrounds. When you open up to cultural interactions, lifelong friendships and a broader perspective await.
- **Self-Discovery Is Part of the Process**: College is not just about academic achievements. It's a transformative journey that allows you to explore new passions, like Aria's love for painting, and discover more about yourself.
- **Balancing Academics and Campus Life**: Finding a balance between your studies and involvement in campus life, whether it's clubs, festivals, or other activities, is essential for a well-rounded college experience.
- **Setting a Solid Academic Foundation**: While college offers myriad experiences, don't forget the primary goal: earning your degree. In the next chapter, we'll explore strategies to ensure academic success.

2 WHY SOME FAIL

You're Not in Kansas Anymore: Why Some College Students Struggle Academically?

In the small town of Kansas, Emily, a young girl with notable academic talents, yearned for more than her familiar, comfortable life. Excelling in every school competition, she dreamt of broader horizons. When she got the chance to attend a prestigious East Coast college, she embraced it eagerly, though not without apprehension about the unknown challenges ahead.

At college, Emily encountered a level of competition and academic rigor she hadn't anticipated. Surrounded by peers as talented as herself and faced with demanding professors, she initially struggled, feeling out of place and questioning her abilities. However, Emily's resilience and determination drove her to seek help, join study groups, and dive deeper into her studies. This proactive approach led to a remarkable academic transformation.

By graduation, Emily had evolved from a small-town prodigy to a confident, accomplished scholar. Her success, reflected in her grades and the respect from her professors and peers, was a testament to her hard work and perseverance. Standing on the graduation stage, Emily realized her achievements were not despite her struggles but because of them. She had proven that success wasn't limited to her small-town origins but was attainable anywhere with persistence and adaptability.

Emily's story highlights the importance of embracing challenges, being open to growth, and the transformative power of perseverance in the face of adversity. Her journey from Kansas to college graduation symbolizes the journey of self-discovery and personal development many students undergo in their academic pursuits.

Why Are You Here? Let's Define Your Purpose

When pondering "Why am I in college?" the initial thought might be earning a degree for career advancement. But college offers more—endless possibilities, sharpening intellect, fostering curiosity, and preparing you for life's unpredictable journey. If your passion for a subject fuels your college path, it's a strong motivator, enhancing creativity and focus. Yet, passion should be balanced with practical, evolving goals. Set SMART goals, maintain a realistic balance in aspirations, and approach big dreams incrementally. College isn't just about a degree; it's a journey of personal growth and a stepping stone to achieving larger life goals. Each challenge you overcome builds resilience, bringing you closer to your ultimate objectives.

Strategies for Setting Effective College Goals

Craft SMART Goals: Define your goals precisely, ensuring they are Specific, Measurable, Achievable, Relevant, and Time-bound. For example, aim for an 'A' in a specific class, like biology, rather than a general desire to excel in the subject.

Maintain a Rhythmic Balance: Set high but realistic aspirations. Balance your academic ambitions with personal well-being to ensure a holistic approach to your college experience.

Dream Big, Act Incrementally: Visualize your ultimate dreams, such as making groundbreaking discoveries or writing a bestseller. Remember, these grand goals are achieved step by step. Start with smaller, achievable objectives that gradually build toward your larger dreams.

Develop Essential Life Skills: College is an ideal place to acquire life skills that will serve you well beyond graduation. Focus on developing skills like time management, critical thinking, teamwork, and effective communication. These skills are pivotal for academic success and crucial in your personal and professional life post-graduation.

Develop Critical Thinking Skills

In a world inundated with information, merely absorbing facts isn't enough. We must cultivate the art of critical thinking—the ability to extract meaning from data in a thoughtful, unbiased, and coherent manner. This cognitive toolkit isn't the exclusive domain of scholars or scientists; it's an essential set of skills for everyone, applicable in myriad contexts, from career choices to civic engagement and daily problem-solving.

So, what does this toolbox of critical thinking entail?

Imagine critical thinking as a collection of mental abilities that empower us to decipher the world around us. The University of Edinburgh defines these skills as the capacity to "identify, scrutinize, and assess arguments and evidence." Let's break down these capabilities:

Observation: This skill involves being keenly aware of your surroundings—identifying patterns, detecting changes, and noticing details others might miss.

Analysis: Think of this as your mental toolkit for unraveling information. It lets you dissect information, discern relation-ships, causes, and effects, and gain deeper insights.

Evaluation: This skill allows you to appraise the reliability of the information at your disposal. It's the tool you wield to determine the credibility and worth of information, argu-ments, or options.

Synthesis: You synthesize the information gathered at this stage, creating a fresh understanding or proposing solutions.

Communication: This involves the ability to express your thoughts in a clear, compelling manner.

How Do You Cultivate Critical Thinking?

Self-Assess Your Decision-Making Process: Dedicate time in your daily routine to review your decisions. Reflect on what you aimed to achieve, the options you considered, the pros and cons of each choice, the information that guided your decision, and the assumptions that influenced it.

Expand Your Perspective: Challenge yourself to see things from different viewpoints. Consider the motives, aspirations, and challenges of others, and engage with individuals who hold diverse experiences and opinions.

Practice Active Listening: Enhance your critical thinking by paying close attention to what others communicate. Show interest and respect through your words and body language, allowing you to understand their message, ask pertinent questions, and provide constructive feedback.

Break Down Your Information: Strive to comprehend the main points, arguments, or evidence in the information you're analyzing. This helps you understand the information's structure, logic, and validity and identify gaps, inconsistencies, or errors in reasoning.

Engage in Research: Seek out and collect relevant information from various sources to broaden your knowledge, challenge your views, and evaluate different information sources.

Nourish Your Curiosity: Cultivate an eagerness to learn and explore new things. Seek fresh information, ask questions, challenge assumptions, and uncover new connections.

Why Critical Thinking Matters

Critical thinking holds a unique allure, doesn't it? Let's peel back the layers and delve into its significance.

Embracing critical thinking encourages you to move beyond accepting facts at face value. Instead, you scrutinize and dissect them, gaining insight into the "how" and "why" of things. This process shapes your perspectives, encourages you to question the status quo, and reveals the myriad shades of life's complexities. Thanks to critical thinking, learning becomes a rich tapestry of wisdom where every morsel enlightens you.

But critical thinking doesn't merely enhance your intelligence; it also nurtures creativity and innovation. It prompts you to venture into uncharted territories, challenge conventions, and unveil innovative solutions. With critical thinking, you're not just a problem solver but also equipped to adapt and thrive in uncertainty. It sharpens your creative faculties, breathing life into your ability to think outside the box.

Critical Thinking in Every Aspect of Life

The essence of critical thinking extends far beyond the classroom. It plays a pivotal role in every facet of life, guiding decision-making and problem-solving. Here are some examples of how critical thinking manifests in various life domains:

College Life: Critical thinking empowers you to assess the reliability of information sources for research papers, dissect complex concepts, and engage in thought-provoking discussions with peers and professors.

First Jobs: In your career, critical thinking aids in problem-solving, decision-making, and innovation. It enables you to evaluate job opportunities, navigate challenges, and contribute fresh ideas to your organization.

Parenting: As a parent, critical thinking helps you make informed choices about your child's education, health, and well-being. It guides you in evaluating parenting advice, making decisions in your family's best interest, and fostering your child's intellectual development.

Travel: When exploring new places, critical thinking assists in planning itineraries, evaluating travel recommendations, and adapting to unexpected situations. It enhances your ability to immerse yourself in local cultures and make the most of your travel experiences.

Financial Planning: In managing finances, critical thinking enables you to analyze investment opportunities, make informed decisions about saving and spending, and plan for long-term financial goals.

Social Interactions: Understanding and empathizing with others, navigating social dynamics, and resolving conflicts.

Media Consumption: Discerning credible sources, understanding biases, and forming independent opinions.

Global Awareness: Interpreting world events, understanding cultural differences, and engaging in civic activities.

Critical thinking is the compass that guides you through life's complex terrain, enriching your experiences, enhancing your problem-solving abilities, and fostering continuous learning and growth.

Time Management and Blocking

The 50-30-20 Formula

Navigating the intricate dance of life, with its multiple dimensions like academics, work, social ties, and personal growth, can often feel like a high-wire act. But fear not; there's a method to bring order to this seeming chaos. Allow me to introduce the 50-30-20 formula, a clever strategy to harmonize your daily pursuits.

Imagine your workday as a delectable pie, divided into three mouthwatering slices. The largest portion, 50%, is reserved for nurturing your long-term aspirations. This is where you invest in your dreams, be it personal development, career planning, or academic endeavors. For instance, if you're charting a course toward becoming a lawyer, half of your day can be dedicated to law studies, online courses, or the pursuit of internships.

The next slice, accounting for 30% of your day, is aimed at mid-term goals, those tasks with looming deadlines in the coming months or years. While they may not directly align with your long-term vision, they serve as stepping stones toward it. If law is your calling, this portion of your day might involve completing assignments, preparing for exams, or networking with future colleagues.

The smallest slice, at 20%, caters to your immediate needs and daily responsibilities. Though they may appear mundane, these tasks are the nuts and bolts of your everyday life. So, if your goal is to grace the courtrooms one day, this fraction of your day could entail checking emails, answering phone calls, or tidying up your study space.

In the grand finale, remember this: The 50-30-20 formula serves as your compass, dividing your time into three harmonious parts—devotion to the future you aspire to (50%), the stepping stones toward it (30%), and the essential tasks of today (20%). Armed with this toolkit, you're well-equipped to orchestrate your life, find balance, and embark confidently on the path to your dreams.

Time Blocking Template

The 50-30-20 formula mentioned earlier could be applied within a time-blocking framework. Here's a table that you can use as a Time Blocking Template tailored to the 50-30-20 rule.

Time Slot	Task Type	Specific Activity	Notes/Goals
8:00 - 12:00	Long-Term Goals (50%)	Studying law-related subjects, taking online courses, etc.	
		Focus on career planning and personal development.	
12:00 - 1:00	Lunch Break		
1:00 - 5:00	Mid-Term Goals (30%)	Completing assignments, preparing for exams, etc.	
		Work on tasks with deadlines within a few months	
5:00 - 5:30	Break/Rest		
5:30 - 7:00	Immediate Goals (20%)	Check emails, return calls, household chores, etc.	
		Daily necessities, short-term tasks	
7:00 - 8:00	Dinner		
8:00 - 10:00	Personal Time	Hobbies, relaxation, etc.	

Please adjust the time slots and specific activities to suit your needs and priorities. You can also expand or contract the different sections based on the time you need for long-term, mid-term, and immediate goals. This table provides a structured way to visualize and organize your day, helping you stay focused and efficient.

As you step into the world of independence, a fresh chapter begins, bringing the need to reshape your family relationships. As you transition to college, discover the ways you can cultivate these connections, ensuring they continue to flourish and support you in this exciting new phase of your life. Keep reading to uncover the art of balancing family bonds as you embark on your academic adventure.

Mastering the art of time organization is potent in your collegiate toolkit, steering you toward achieving personal and academic aspirations. Balancing academic demands, social commitments, distractions, and the allure of procrastination can feel like a Herculean task. In this section, we'll explore the world of effective time management and introduce you to "hour structuring," which can empower you to craft and utilize your time precisely.

Unlocking the Benefits of Time Mastery

Mastery of time offers a range of rewards:

Enhanced Academic Success: Proficient time management skills can be your secret weapon, helping you meet deadlines, prepare for assessments, and avoid last-minute panic. This often results in improved grades and a deeper grasp of knowledge.

Stress Reduction: Effective time organization enables you to sidestep the last-minute rush and anxiety, allowing you to handle deadlines and expectations gracefully. This can translate into reduced stress and a greater sense of accomplishment.

Increased Productivity: Time mastery lets you accomplish more in less time. You can focus on the most critical tasks while minimizing disruptions and distractions, enhancing efficiency and work quality.

Improved Well-being: Effective time management maintains a healthy balance between academic responsibilities and personal life, ensuring ample time for health, hobbies, relationships, and leisure. This contributes to better physical, mental, and emotional well-being.

Structuring Your Hours—A Technique for Time Mastery

Structuring your hours involves dividing your day into blocks of time, each dedicated to a specific task or activity. The concept is built on the idea that planning and organization of your hours can fine-tune your focus, drive, and productivity. While this technique can be customized to your unique needs and goals, here's a general outline to guide you:

Focus on Goals: Identify your short-term and long-term academic and personal goals. Be specific and express them clearly.

Goal Breakdown: Divide your goals into manageable, bite-sized tasks or steps needed for achievement.

Time Estimation: Estimate the time required for each task realistically, considering your abilities, resources, and constraints. Timing your tasks can be helpful in this process.

Create a Schedule: Develop a schedule or calendar that assigns each task to a specific time block. Include your classes, work hours, meals, breaks, and other commitments in your schedule.

Stick to the Schedule: Make an effort to adhere to your schedule, focusing on the task at hand until completion or the end of the time block.

Schedule Review: Evaluate your schedule at the end of each day or week, identifying strengths and areas for improvement.

Tips for Effective Time Block Utilization

As you structure your hours in college, consider these tips:

Flexibility: Adjust your schedule when necessary, allowing for unexpected changes and emergencies.

Realism: Avoid overloading every moment with tasks. Allocate buffer time for transitions or unforeseen delays and some free time for relaxation.

Consistency: Establish a routine that suits you and follow it regularly with minor adjustments. This can help you develop habits and save time.

Clarity: Define your goal in each time block to maintain focus and motivation.

By mastering the art of time organization and utilizing the hour structuring technique, you can navigate the complexities of college life with greater ease and efficiency.

Making Your Schedule Visible and Accessible

Structuring your hours and managing your time effectively involves more than just creating a schedule—it's also crucial to keep that schedule visible and accessible. Here are some tips on how to do it:

- **Digital vs. Physical:** Decide whether you prefer digital scheduling apps or a physical planner. Both have their advantages, so choose the one that works best for you.
- **Color Coding:** Use color-coding techniques to distinguish between different types of tasks or commitments. For example, use one color for classes, another for work, and another for personal time.
- **Sync Devices:** If you use digital tools, make sure to sync your schedule across all your devices—computer, smartphone, and tablet. This ensures you can access your schedule anytime, anywhere.
- **Display It:** If you opt for a physical planner, keep it in a visible place in your dorm room or study area. A wall calendar with your schedule can serve as a daily reminder.
- **Set Reminders:** Use alarms and reminders on your devices to prompt you when it's time to transition between tasks or activities.
- **Share with Accountability Partners:** If you have study partners or accountability buddies, consider

sharing your schedule with them. This can help you stay on track and support each other's productivity.

- **Regular Updates:** Regardless of your scheduling method, remember to update it regularly to reflect any changes in your commitments or priorities.
- **Accessibility Tools:** Explore apps and tools designed for individuals with ADHD or organizational challenges. These tools often include features like visual schedules and reminders.

By making your schedule visible and accessible, you'll enhance your ability to stick to it and make the most of your structured hours. This practice can significantly contribute to your academic success and overall well-being.

Remember that effective time management is an ongoing process, and finding the right strategies and tools that work for you may take some experimentation. Stay flexible, adapt your schedule as needed, and keep striving for productivity and balance in your college life.

Avoiding procrastination

Procrastination is a term that likely strikes a chord with you. It's like a mysterious shadow that hovers around college campuses, ready to trap unsuspecting students. While it may seem like an inevitable part of student life, it's more akin to a puzzle waiting to be solved with the right approach. Let's discover how to outsmart this formidable obstacle and regain control of your academic journey.

Igniting Interest in Mundane Tasks

Now, what about those seemingly dull, uninspiring tasks? Lack of interest can often be the culprit behind procrastination. However, you can infuse purpose into even the most mundane endeavors with a dash of creativity. It might be about personal satisfaction, the opportunity to learn something new, or the excitement of achieving a top-notch grade. Remind yourself of the benefits, and you'll uncover that spark that rekindles your motivation.

Taming the Temptation of Distractions

Ah, distractions, the crafty seducers of productivity! Social media, friends, food, and sleep can beckon to you like sirens at sea. To resist their allure, create an environment that resembles a personal study haven. Power down those electronic devices, seek a cozy, distraction-free spot, or surround yourself with focused peers. Transform your study routine into an engaging treasure hunt, and you'll develop greater resistance to these common distractions.

Navigating the Waters of Disorganization

Disorganization and confusion can cast a spell of procrastination. If you ever find yourself adrift in a sea of information, it's time to become the captain of your study ship. Gather your materials, clarify instructions, and deploy tools that are trusty navigational aids. Calendars, planners, or specialized apps can become your steadfast allies in this quest for clarity and order.

Remember, procrastination isn't an impossible curse; it's a habit that can be reshaped and refined. These strategies are your magical keys to unlock a more productive and joyful college experience. Allow them to guide you, and you'll discover that procrastination becomes a myth of the past, enabling you to embrace the exhilarating learning adventure fully. With these newfound skills, you'll set sail toward academic success with the wind at your back and the open sea of knowledge before you.

Strategies for Balancing Academic and Social Life

Prioritize Tasks: Clearly distinguish between urgent/important tasks and social activities.

Set Clear Boundaries: Allocate specific times for studying and socializing. Stick to these schedules.

Use a Planner: Organize your tasks and social events in a planner to visualize and manage your time effectively.

Study Groups: Combine socializing with studying by forming or joining study groups.

Reward System: Reward yourself with social activities after completing study goals.

Digital Tools: Utilize apps that help track tasks and limit social media use during study hours.

Mindfulness Practices: Engage in mindfulness to stay focused and reduce the urge to procrastinate.

Regular Breaks: Take short breaks during study sessions to refresh and avoid burnout.

Set Realistic Goals: Avoid overcommitting; set achievable study and social goals.

Reflect on Consequences: Consider the long-term impact of procrastination on academic goals.

Balancing Priorities: Essential Skills for College and Beyond

In college, learning to balance academic responsibilities with a buzzing social life is about more than just immediate success; it's a crucial life skill. The ability to effectively prioritize during college lays a strong foundation for your future, especially in professional settings where distractions and demands on your time are constant. By mastering the art of prioritization and tactfully managing social commitments, you develop a skill set that ensures success beyond the university gates. It enables you to navigate life's varied challenges, maintain focus on your goals, and achieve a fulfilling and organized life. This includes learning to politely decline or exit social situations, a skill equally valuable in professional environments.

Politely declining or exiting social situations requires tact and honesty.

Here are some strategies:

Honesty with Tact: Be honest about your need to focus on your studies but express it tactfully. For example, "I'd love to join, but I have an important exam to prepare for."

Offer Alternatives: Suggest an alternative time for socializing. For instance, "I can't make it tonight, but how about we catch up this weekend?"

Use Positive Language: Frame your refusal positively, like, "I'm really committed to acing this project right now, but let's plan something soon!"

Short and Sweet: Keep your response brief and to the point, avoiding over-explanation.

Gratitude: Show appreciation for the invitation, "Thanks for thinking of me! I wish I could join."

Set Priorities: Occasionally remind your friends of your priorities so they understand your commitments.

Quick Exit Strategy: If you're already at an event, excuse yourself politely, perhaps saying you have an early day or study plans.

3 FROM FRESHMAN TO FINISH LINE

Books are your trusty sidekicks for anyone stepping into the vast universe of knowledge that is a college education. Like the beat of a hummingbird's wing, they flit about, filled with the nectar of wisdom, skills, bursts of inspiration, a good laugh when you need one, and often a shoulder to lean on in the form of motivation.

However, there's a different side to this coin. Books, especially those necessary to feed the academic beast, aren't always gentle on your pocket. This doesn't mean your learning journey should suffer. There are multiple paths to owning those all-important texts without emptying your bank account.

Acquiring Textbooks Without Breaking the Bank

Go Digital:

- Before you commit your dollars to that textbook, why not take a moment to explore the virtual marketplace? Websites and applications exist to help you compare book prices from various vendors. Think Amazon, Chegg, AbeBooks, and BookFinder. Let's not forget about price trackers, too. CamelCamelCamel or Honey are perfect assistants that watch price histories, alerting you when prices sink, or a sale is on. This digital exercise could be your key to great savings and free time.

Secondhand Doesn't Mean Second-Best:

- An effective strategy to save your pennies is to go for used books. Sure, they're not brand new, but often in good shape. Specialized websites such as ThriftBooks, Better World Books, and Alibris are brimming with secondhand books waiting for a new home. Or you could turn to fellow students who have walked the path you are on now. Social media, online forums, bulletin boards, or even a chat over coffee could land you some used books at affordable prices.

The Older Edition Advantage:

- The latest edition of a book isn't always the superior one. Older versions are often just as good and considerably lighter on the wallet. But check with your professor if using older editions will serve your purpose. Professors sometimes insist on the latest edition for their updated content. If you get a thumbs up for older editions, double-check the layout—page numbers, chapters, sections—to ensure they align with the newest edition.

Share and Care:

- Have you considered getting your hands on those books without spending a dime? It's doable. Your school library could be a treasure chest of textbooks you need. Borrow, use, return. Rinse and repeat. And then there's the idea of sharing with your classmates. Cost-sharing a book or an exchange system can work wonders. Plus, it opens up avenues for group study and learning from each other.

Exploring Low-Cost and Free Alternatives:

- If owning books feels too heavy on the pocket, you could explore low-cost or free alternatives.
- Digital Copies or Alternative Editions: Some generous authors or publishers might offer digital

versions or different editions of their books for free or at a fraction of the cost of the printed versions.

- Open Educational Resources (OER): This is a world of teaching and learning resources open to anyone with internet access. It's a universe where textbooks, courses, videos, podcasts, and simulations coexist for free use, modification, and sharing. Websites like OpenStax, OER Commons, and MERLOT are your gateways to this world.

- Library Databases: Your school library might have access to databases housing academic journals, articles, ebooks, and more. These can be the perfect supplement or even replacements for your textbooks.

- Course Reserves: Your professor might put some books on reserve in your school library. These high-demand or pricey books are for your use within the library for a limited period.

The price tag of books needn't weigh down the journey of a college student. There are many secret paths to owning the books you need for your courses without draining your finances. From exploring digital options and secondhand sources to embracing older editions and sharing with classmates, these tips and strategies ensure you can have and read your books without duplicating efforts or information.

Study Methods

Unleashing your brain's full capacity for learning can become your secret superpower in academics. Yet, many grapple with finding the golden key to unlock their ability to absorb, process, and remember information for their coursework and exams. Since the landscape of learning styles is as diverse as our fingerprints, finding a universal key is unrealistic. However, we can forge some versatile tools to aid our quest for knowledge. Let's shine a light on some of these tools.

Experience the Pomodoro Study Technique

This time management approach offers a remarkable solution by promoting short, concentrated periods of effort interspersed with brief moments of relaxation. The rhythm of work and rest boosts your mental agility, drive, and effectiveness. Sounds exciting? All you need is a timer, a writing instrument, and paper. Here is the path to undertake:

First, pick a task or topic that's on your study list. Launch your timer for a set duration of 25 minutes and engage fully with your study material. Stay committed to your work, dodging distractions that might arise. When your timer buzzes, it's time to pause. Put a tick on your paper indicating a completed study burst, and step into a 5-minute rest interval. This is your opportunity to stretch, hydrate, or do something soothing.

Continue to replicate this rhythm until you have accumulated four Pomodoros—translating to 100 minutes of dedicated work with 15 minutes of relaxation. Post four Pomodoros, indulge in an extended break of 15 to 30 minutes. This time, gift yourself with an enjoyable activity. Carry forward this cycle with the next task on your list until you reach the end of your study session.

The beauty of the Pomodoro technique is that it actively discourages exhaustion, monotony, and weariness that often accompany extensive study sessions. Additionally, it offers a tangible means to track your progress and utilize your time effectively.

Let's Understand the Feynman Technique

Turning our attention to another effective study tool, we have the Feynman technique. This method strengthens your grasp of intricate concepts and amplifies your communication skills. Named after Richard Feynman, a recipient of the Nobel Prize in Physics, this technique is renowned for its simplicity in explaining abstract ideas. The Feynman technique's underlying principle is that teaching something to someone else fosters superior learning. By taking on the mantle of a teacher, you can spot any holes or misconceptions in your understanding and develop ways to simplify and demystify them. Here's how you can implement the Feynman Technique:

Select a concept that you wish to comprehend better. Visualize that you are explaining it to someone unfamiliar with the subject matter. This person could be a friend, a relative, or a fictitious entity. The key is to describe the concept in straightforward language, deploying practical examples or diagrams when required. Remember to abstain from using technical terms or complicated formulas. Once your explanation is ready, scrutinize it to identify any segments you find difficult to explain lucidly. Refer to your source material for additional information or examples to fill these gaps. Keep iterating through this process until you can confidently and precisely articulate the concept.

The Feynman technique is a powerful tool that deepens your understanding of any subject and boosts your critical thinking and problem-solving capabilities. It's particularly beneficial when preparing for exams, presentations, or interviews, as it enhances your ability to express yourself clearly and succinctly.

The Power of Mind Mapping

The final study tool in this section (not the least by any means) that you can add to your repertoire is mind mapping. It is a strategy that utilizes words and images to craft strong associations to aid your recall of the study material. Many find mind mapping a more intuitive form of note-taking, as it can be employed for brainstorming, planning, summarizing, and more.

The premise of mind mapping rests on the theory that our brains better absorb information when presented in a visual and creative format instead of a linear, logical structure. By employing colors, symbols, pictures, and keywords, you can capture and organize your ideas in a manner that resonates with you and stimulates your creativity.

To create a mind map:

Begin with a central topic or idea that encapsulates your aim to learn or study.

Add branches from the center, each representing subtopics or keywords linked to the main topic.

Expand these branches further to include more details or examples as required. You can also incorporate images, icons, or doodles to illustrate your points or trigger your memory.

Mind mapping can bolster your memory, creativity, and comprehension while studying. It also helps you perceive the overall image and the links between distinct concepts or topics. You can craft mind maps manually using paper and pens or opt for online platforms that offer more features and flexibility. Online tools enable you to modify, share, and collaborate on your mind maps and export them in PDF, Word, or PowerPoint formats. Visit Biggerplate at http://www.biggerplate.com/ for a wealth of resources, templates, and tutorials to supercharge your learning and organization.

Remember that different techniques may resonate more with certain subjects or scenarios. So, don't stop experimenting with them and discovering what aligns best with your learning style.

Practical Application vs. Active Reading

As you embark on your academic journey, you'll be surrounded by a vast sea of text. These written works, whether textbooks, essays, reports, or captivating novels, hold the keys to your kingdom of knowledge. Every word, sentence, and paragraph within these texts offer valuable insights, honing your ability to think critically, analyze deeply, and communicate effectively. But here's the twist – not every text reveals its secrets similarly. That's where our discussion on reading strategies comes in, particularly practical application and active reading.

The practical application serves as a bridge, connecting the theoretical wisdom you gain from texts to the practical realities of life. It's about transforming textual knowledge into a practical tool you can confidently wield in the real world. With practical application, the text springs to life, enhancing your motivation, piquing your interest, and elevating the overall joy of reading.

Consider these scenarios:

Utilizing a mathematical concept or formula from a textbook to solve a real-world problem.

Crafting a persuasive email to a government official using the logic and evidence you've gleaned from an article.

Creating a product or service based on the instructions or principles found in a manual.

Performing a scene from a play to bring the characters and themes envisioned by the author to life.

Now, let's venture into the realm of active reading. This strategy invites you to engage intimately with the text. It's a deliberate dance where you interact with each line, enhancing your comprehension, retention, and analytical skills. Active reading sharpens your focus, boosts your memory, and empowers you to form well-grounded opinions.

Here are some active reading techniques to consider:

- Developing a repertoire of questions to ask before, during, and after reading, delving into the text's purpose, core ideas, and finer details.
- Taking notes with thoughts, summaries, or assessments in the margins crystallizes your understanding.
- Creating visual aids like outlines or flowcharts to better visualize and organize the presented information.
- Formulate your examination questions based on the text to put your understanding to the test.
- Sharing the knowledge you've gathered from the text with someone else to solidify your understanding and uncover any gaps.

Neither practical application nor active reading is a one-size-fits-all solution. As you navigate your academic journey, you'll discover that each text or situation may require a different approach. Therefore, remaining flexible, adaptable, and open to various reading techniques is crucial. By doing so, you'll find yourself reading, absorbing, and growing with every word you encounter.

Conquering Exams and Tests: Techniques for Effective Exam Preparation and Performance

Exams and tests are a significant part of the college experience, and your success in these assessments can greatly impact your overall academic performance. To conquer exams and tests effectively, you need a strategic approach that combines preparation, time management, and stress management. This section will delve into techniques to help you excel in your exams and perform at your best when it matters most.

Understand the Exam Format

One of the first steps in preparing for an exam is to thoroughly understand the format. Are you facing multiple-choice questions, essays, short answers, or a combination of these? Knowing what to expect can help you tailor your study plan accordingly. Review any guidelines or rubrics provided by your professor.

Create a Study Schedule

Effective exam preparation begins with a well-structured study schedule. Start early to avoid last-minute cramming, which can lead to stress and decreased retention. Allocate specific time slots for each subject or topic, and be consistent in your study routine. This helps distribute your workload and prevents burnout.

Organize Your Study Material

Organize your study materials, notes, and resources to streamline your review process. Create clear and concise study guides or outlines for each subject or topic. Highlight key concepts, formulas, and definitions. Use color-coding or visual aids to make information more memorable.

Practice Active Learning

Passive reading and highlighting are not as effective as active learning techniques. Engage with the material by summarizing, questioning, and teaching it to yourself or others. Solve practice problems, write sample essays, and participate in study groups to reinforce your understanding.

Use Memory Techniques

Employ memory techniques such as mnemonic devices, acronyms, and visualization to enhance memory retention. Break down complex information into smaller, manageable chunks. Spaced repetition, where you review material at increasing intervals, is also an effective memory-enhancing strategy.

Take Practice Exams

Practice exams or mock tests are invaluable for assessing your knowledge and improving test-taking skills. Use past exam papers or online resources to simulate exam conditions. Time yourself to gauge your pace and identify areas where you need improvement.

Stay Healthy and Manage Stress

A healthy lifestyle plays a significant role in exam preparation. Get adequate sleep, maintain a balanced diet, and exercise regularly. Managing stress through relaxation techniques like deep breathing, meditation, or yoga can help you stay focused and calm during exams.

Foods to Boost Focus During Studying and Test-Taking

In addition to the techniques mentioned above, your diet can play a crucial role in enhancing concentration and mental clarity during studying and test-taking. Incorporate these brain-boosting foods into your routine:

Blueberries: Packed with antioxidants, blueberries improve memory and cognitive function. They are a perfect snack for study breaks.

Fatty Fish: Salmon, mackerel, and trout are rich in omega-3 fatty acids, which support brain health. They enhance memory and help maintain focus.

Dark Chocolate: Dark chocolate contains antioxidants and

caffeine, which can improve alertness and mood. Enjoy a small piece as a treat during study sessions.

Nuts and Seeds: Almonds, walnuts, and flaxseeds provide essential nutrients like vitamin E and omega-3s. They promote clear thinking and memory retention.

Leafy Greens: Spinach, kale, and other leafy greens are high in vitamins and minerals. They boost cognitive function and protect the brain from age-related decline.

Whole Grains: Opt for whole grains like oats and quinoa, which release glucose slowly into the bloodstream. This provides a steady supply of energy to the brain.

Berries: Strawberries, raspberries, and blackberries are rich in antioxidants and vitamin C. They help reduce stress and improve cognitive performance.

Avocado: Avocado is a source of healthy fats that support brain function. It also contains potassium, which enhances memory and concentration.

Turmeric: Curcumin, found in turmeric, has anti-inflamma-tory and antioxidant properties. It may improve memory and reduce brain fog.

Green Tea: Green tea contains L-theanine, an amino acid that promotes relaxation and focus without causing drowsiness.

Remember to stay hydrated by drinking plenty of water throughout your study sessions and exam days. Avoid excessive caffeine intake, which can lead to jitteriness and disrupt sleep. Instead, use herbal teas like chamomile or peppermint to stay calm and alert.

Incorporating these brain-boosting foods into your diet can enhance your cognitive abilities, improve focus, and support your overall academic success. Combine these dietary choices with effective study techniques and stress management strategies for optimal exam performance.

You Can Do So Much With Tutoring

Have you ever stumbled upon a hidden gem in the most unexpected places? Well, that's what tutoring is all about – uncovering hidden potentials. It's like a journey of self-discovery, where you unlock the treasures of knowledge hidden within you. But who are the wizards behind this magical process? They come in all forms – professors, fellow students, experts, and even volunteers – each with their unique way of making complex subjects seem as easy as pie.

Tutoring can happen anywhere – online, in the comfort of your dorm room, on the bustling campus, or even within small study groups where the energy is contagious.

Now, let's clear up a common misconception. Tutoring isn't the same as teaching. Teaching covers many topics, while tutoring serves bite-sized portions, focusing only on your needs. Are those math problems starting to resemble secret codes? Do you want to boost your grades or just need some extra practice? Think of tutoring as a tailor-made learning experience designed just for you.

The fascinating thing about tutoring is its flexibility. There are different styles to suit your preferences. In one-on-one tutoring, you take the center stage. Here, the pace of learning is entirely up to you, ensuring that the lessons are perfectly tailored to your unique needs. It's like having a custom-made suit of knowledge that fits you perfectly. And whether you prefer face-to-face interactions or virtual sessions, the choice is yours.

Then there's group tutoring. Imagine a small group of students, all with the same academic goals, learning together. This approach is fantastic if you enjoy studying with peers, love teamwork, or are mindful of your budget. Depending on what suits you best, you can choose between digital or in-person group sessions.

Peer tutoring is another interesting twist. Picture a fellow student, someone who's been in your shoes, sharing their wisdom. This helps ease the stress of exams and encourages active participation. These sessions often take place on campus or in the vast online realm.

Finding the right tutoring group might seem like a daunting task. But fear not! The digital world offers a plethora of possibilities. And don't forget to tap into your social network – your school, friends, and family might have excellent recommendations. When weighing your options, consider a few key factors – cost, quality, convenience, flexibility, and feedback.

Tutoring isn't just a service; it's a powerful tool. It bolsters your academic arsenal, taking you straight toward your learning goals. Once you discover the right tutoring group, you'll have an invaluable companion on your quest for knowledge. Plus, it adds a sprinkle of much-needed fun to the learning process. Who said learning can't be both work and play?

Knock Their Socks Off With a Well-Written College Paper!

Writing Winning College Papers

Ah, college papers—the classic academic challenge that beckons every student on their educational journey. Whether it's a research paper, an essay, or a critical analysis, mastering the art of writing these assignments can be a game-changer in your college experience. While it may seem daunting at first, rest assured that with the right strategies, anyone can become proficient at crafting well-researched, eloquent papers that not only earn top grades but also showcase your intellect and analytical skills. This chapter will explore the key steps to help you confidently conquer your college papers.

Crafting a Clear and Concise Thesis Statement

Every outstanding college paper commences with a crisp, direct thesis statement—an illuminating guide that steers your reader through your argument. Your thesis should encapsulate the core concept of your paper within a single sentence, serving as the linchpin that maintains your writing's focus and coherence.

To fashion an effective thesis statement, adhere to these principles:

Be Precise: Steer clear of vague statements; precisely identify the subject of your paper.

Quantify Your Claim: Your thesis should present a stance that is open to examination and assessment.

Keep It Feasible: Ensure your thesis is attainable within the parameters of your paper.

Relevance Is Paramount: The thesis should directly pertain to your topic.

Establish a Timeline: If pertinent, define a timeframe for your argument within the paper.

2. Back Up Your Thesis Statement

Once you've established your thesis, your paper's body serves as the support structure for your argument. Each paragraph should provide evidence, examples, and analysis to validate your thesis statement. This is where critical thinking skills come into play as you dissect your chosen topic, consider various perspectives, and provide well-researched evidence to strengthen your position.

3. Build an Outline

Before diving headfirst into writing, create a well-structured outline. Outlining helps you organize your thoughts, ensuring that your paper flows logically. Start with a strong introduction, then body paragraphs discussing a distinct point, and conclude with a compelling summary of your main arguments.

4. The First Draft

Don't agonize over achieving perfection in your initial draft. The primary purpose of this stage is to get your ideas down on paper. Write freely, and don't fret over minor errors or language intricacies. Once your thoughts are on the page, you can revise and refine them.

5. Write the Introduction Last

Although the introduction is the first part of your paper that your reader encounters, it's often best to write it last. By waiting until you've completed the body of your paper, you can craft an introduction that accurately reflects the content and direction of your essay.

In your introduction, aim to:

Engage the Reader: Use a captivating hook to pique your reader's interest.

Provide Context: Offer background information to contextualize your topic.

State Your Thesis: Present your thesis statement.

Outline Your Approach: Briefly describe how your paper will unfold.

6. Editing and Proofreading

After completing your first draft, step back and give yourself some time before revising. This break allows you to return to your work with fresh eyes, making it easier to spot errors, inconsistencies, and areas for improvement. During the editing process:

Check for Clarity: Ensure your ideas are clearly expressed, and your argument flows logically.

Refine Your Language: Eliminate unnecessary words, use precise vocabulary, and vary sentence structure to enhance readability.

Review Grammar and Style: Pay attention to punctuation, grammar, and formatting rules.

Seek Feedback: Consider sharing your paper with a peer or professor for constructive criticism.

While AI tools can be beneficial for obtaining suggestions and feedback during the editing process, it's essential to clarify that they should never be used to generate the paper from start to finish. AI can aid in enhancing your work, but it should complement your writing, not replace it.

7. Citation and References

College papers often require citing sources to support your arguments. Be sure to follow the citation style specified by your instructor, whether it's APA, MLA, Chicago, or another format. Keep meticulous records of your sources and their page numbers to facilitate proper citation.

8. Proofreading and Final Touches

Before submitting your paper, conduct a final proofread. Carefully examine grammar, spelling, and punctuation. You can also utilize tools like Grammarly or other websites that help you identify common grammar issues. Ensure your paper follows formatting guidelines, such as margins, font size, and line spacing. Additionally, double-check that your citations are accurate and complete. This meticulous review ensures that your paper is polished and ready for submission.

9. Seek feedback

Don't hesitate to contact professors, tutors, or writing centers for guidance and feedback. Constructive criticism can immensely benefit your writing and help you refine your skills.

10. Conclusion

Writing winning college papers is a skill that takes time to develop. Still, with practice and dedication, you can master it. Remember that each paper you write is an opportunity to showcase your critical thinking, research prowess, and communication ability. Embrace the writing process, and you'll earn top grades and gain valuable skills that will serve you well throughout your academic and professional journey.

Walking Tall in College

Imagine yourself in a college classroom, your heart fluttering like a bird poised for its inaugural flight, palms slightly damp. The room thrums with intellectual prowess, the aura of accomplishment almost palpable. Suddenly, uncertainty taps your shoulder. Is this environment truly for you? Are you capable of tackling these challenges and flourishing? Banish that fear, dear reader, for your potential is boundless; you just need a sprinkle of academic confidence.

The Essence of Academic Confidence

Forget buzzwords; academic confidence is your magic carpet, lifting you above mountains of academic challenges. It fuels motivation, engagement, performance, and personal wellness in college. It protects against anxiety, stress, laziness, avoidance, and poor results. The million-dollar question arises: how do you acquire this potent potion of success?

1. Self and Peer Assessment

Embrace self-assessment as the camera that throws back your progress in high definition. Pair it with peer assessment. Together, they offer a clear lens that enhances your academic vision, providing insights into your strengths, weaknesses, and opportunities for growth.

2. Constructive Feedback

Feedback isn't meant to reduce your efforts to rubble but to build bridges from your current state to your could-be excellence. Seek timely, specific, balanced, actionable, and respectful feedback, and watch your academic confidence take flight.

3. Clearing the Mental Clutter

Allow your mind some breathing space. Bid farewell to self-doubt, anxiety, stress, guilt, and shame. Breathe in positivity via exercises like meditation, journaling, or seeking trusted confidants. Create a space for creativity and problem-solving, and let the radiance of confidence pierce through.

4. Positivity: Your Shield Against Negativity

Arm yourself with positivity, your shield against negativity from various sources. Replace doubts with affirmations, confront critics gracefully, and tackle stress like a seasoned warrior.

5. The Power of Vulnerability

Recognize that seeking help is not a sign of weakness but a display of strength. Let guidance, encouragement, and advice be your allies in the battleground of academia. Your growth and confidence will be better for it.

6. Micro-Confidence: The Building Blocks of Success

Cherish the small but significant acts that constitute micro-confidence. They are the building blocks of a towering edifice of self-assurance, resilience, and success.

7. Nurturing Pride

Plant seeds of achievements and water them with appreciation. Witness them bloom into a lush garden of motivation, satisfaction, and confidence.

8. Aligning With Passion

Align your academic path with your values, interests, and passions. Let them be your guide, leading you toward fulfillment and joy.

You are now armed with the tools to tackle the college experience with academic confidence as your guide. Employ these techniques and watch your transformation into a confident scholar, prepared to explore, learn, and conquer. Your college success story is yours to write; the pen is in your hand. Create your masterpiece.

Forming friendships, connecting with professors and tutors, and weaving yourself into the colorful fabric of college life—these do not have to be a struggle. If the initial chapters haven't quite drawn you into the joyful dance of campus living, perhaps this third attempt will strike the right chord and guide you into the rhythm of academic enjoyment.

4   FINDING YOUR VOICE

THE ONLY JOURNEY IS THE ONE WITHIN. –
RAINER MARIA RILKE

Navigating the college campus can sometimes make forming connections feel like venturing into uncharted territory. As you look around, it might seem like everyone else has effortlessly found their place, leaving you feeling like a puzzle piece that doesn't quite fit. Surprisingly, this sense of unease is quite common, with approximately 53% of students sharing these feelings (according to Gen Z College, 2022). But there's no need to worry. This chapter serves as your reliable guide to creating genuine connections and engaging in meaningful conversations. Within these pages, you'll uncover the art of forging friendships that flow as naturally as breathing. Armed with the insights found here, you'll nurture connections that not only fill your social landscape but also enrich your life, transforming moments of solitude into a beautiful symphony of friendships and meaningful encounters.

Vanquishing Social Isolation

Emily stood at the threshold of a brand-new chapter in her life, her dorm room symbolizing endless possibilities. College felt like an exciting adventure with a mix of excitement, a touch of uncertainty, and just a hint of nerves. As she looked around at her unfamiliar surroundings, her heart raced with anticipation. College, with its vast landscape, beckoned to her, an introvert ready to tackle its challenges.

During her early college days, Emily became a devoted bookworm and a curious learner. Her room was like a library, filled with the well-loved scent of novels. While her peers were out making friends, her companions were the characters from her favorite books. Her happiness was a solitary one, shared only with the authors of those beloved stories. But as she watched her lively classmates effortlessly making connections, something inside her stirred—a deep desire to be a part of that tapestry of relationships.

Her adventurous spirit led her to a book club, where she felt a bit hesitant at first but soon found fellow book lovers who shared her passion. It was like watching a hidden flower slowly bloom, finding its place among kindred souls. Yet, some nights brought a sense of solitude to Emily. While others reveled in joy and laughter, she sometimes felt the pull of loneliness, aware that she was still within her self-imposed boundaries. But Emily was determined to break free. She reached out to others, starting with a simple coffee date with her roommate, which turned into an afternoon of revelations and shared dreams. That coffee date marked the beginning of a beautiful friendship.

Before long, an invitation to a party arrived, a beacon of light in the midst of her hesitation. Parties were uncharted territory for Emily, but wasn't college all about exploring the unknown? Encouraged by her newfound friend, she not only picked out an outfit but also gathered newfound courage. Stepping into the party felt like turning a page in her life's story. Amidst the noise and chaos, Emily discovered kindred spirits—fellow introverts, each a unique note in a symphony of shared moments. They talked, laughed, and intertwined their lives. Weeks turned into cherished memories, and Emily began to bloom. Her connections, though few, were deep and meaningful. Solitude was gradually replaced by a sense of belonging. She found her rhythm, her melody, and, most importantly, she found herself.

For Emily, college wasn't just a series of hallways or a class schedule; it was a vast canvas, and she was its artist. She was ready to infuse her world with color, one inspired brushstroke at a time.

Solitude: An Oasis and a Mirage

Discovering the beauty of spending time alone is like finding your favorite tune—a peaceful rhythm of self-reflection, relaxation, and getting to know yourself better. Dive into the enchanting world of a good book, the comfort of your favorite songs, or the joy of pursuing your hobbies solo. Your personal space can become a cozy and empowering retreat.

But, it's important to navigate this path carefully because too much alone time can sometimes lead to isolation. College is all about growth and new experiences, and those experiences often come from interactions with others. While enjoying your "me time" is great, you don't want it to become a wall that keeps you from connecting with people.

It's reassuring to know that many students, just like you, go through similar feelings. Understanding that loneliness is something many people experience can be the first step in finding a balance and reducing some of the stress that comes with it. Feeling a bit out of place in a new environment is perfectly normal.

So, don't hesitate to reach out and start a conversation. You might be surprised to find that your seemingly quiet neighbor or the person eating alone in the cafeteria is also looking for social connections. By sharing your thoughts and experiences, you can build strong bonds and turn your college journey into a harmonious ensemble, rather than a solo performance.

The Power of Groups and New Interests

College is a vibrant stage, brimming with opportunities to participate in group activities and explore new hobbies. These platforms serve as your golden tickets, leading you to potential comrades and the chance to forge meaningful friendships. Whether it's joining a sports team, participating in a drama group, or getting involved in a charity organization, engaging in these spaces can connect you with individuals who resonate with your interests.

Don't hesitate to experiment and step outside of your comfort zone. College serves as the ideal rehearsal ground for venturing into uncharted territories. You may find that the most unlikely pursuits can ignite your passion and lead you toward unexpected and enriching friendships.

Reach Out to Your Cheer Squad

Distance doesn't diminish the significance of your relationships back home. Your family and friends continue to be your enthusiastic supporters, even when miles separate you. Thanks to technology, the world feels smaller than ever, allowing you to maintain the vitality of your cherished bonds through regular calls, video chats, or heartfelt text messages.

These connections offer solace, guidance, and a stable anchor during moments of solitude, enabling you to navigate the challenges of college life.

Facing solitude in college can initially seem like a daunting solo performance. However, it has the potential to evolve into an enriching ensemble experience with the right approach. Embracing solitude without losing your sense of self, recognizing that others share similar feelings, exploring various groups and hobbies, sharing your interests with peers, and staying connected with your support system back home can transform the initial apprehension into a harmonious and fulfilling melody.

Check-Ins: Staying Connected

The college journey marks not just a change in scenery but a transformation in the dynamics of family life. As college students explore new horizons, face challenges, and experience personal growth, their parents also embark on a journey of their own, shifting from caregivers to supportive advisors. The physical distance that often separates families, spanning cities, states, or even countries, need not create an emotional divide. On the contrary, it offers an enriching opportunity to redefine and strengthen the parent-child connection.

But how can you navigate this change effectively? Allow me to guide you through this process.

Communication: It's not merely about routine conversations; it's about meaningful exchanges of emotions, achievements, struggles, and words of encouragement. Striking the right balance between quality and frequency is essential, whether through heartfelt phone calls, thoughtful emails, or lively video chats. It's about more than just talking; it's about truly connecting, understanding, and bridging the miles between you.

Visits: These are not just opportunities to see each other but moments of shared experiences, understanding, laughter, and love. Planning visits requires more than coordination; it demands flexibility, openness, and a genuine eagerness to immerse yourself in each other's worlds, whether on a bustling college campus or in the comfort of your hometown.

Celebrations: Special occasions are not mere dates on a calendar; they are milestones filled with love, pride, joy, and lasting memories. Thoughtfully commemorating these moments through heartfelt gifts, virtual gatherings, or in-person festivities contributes to a shared history and a continued sense of unity.

These strategies are not just methods but pathways to nurturing a deeper, more meaningful connection. While physical separation may initially appear challenging and stressful, it does not have to be a barrier. With open hearts, a willingness to adapt, and an eagerness to connect, parents and students can build a relationship that not only endures but flourishes. Embrace this transition with grace, wisdom, and hope, for the distance that may feel like a gap today can be the very thing that brings you closer tomorrow.

Navigating College Relationships

Amidst the vibrant whirlwind of college life, the friendships you cultivate become not only your steadfast anchor but also the pillars of your support system. These bonds infuse your college journey with companionship, laughter, and inspiration, motivating you to excel academically while enhancing your overall social and emotional well-being.

However, it's essential to recognize that not every college friendship is akin to a four-leaf clover. Some relationships may prove unhealthy, toxic, superficial, or misaligned with your personal goals and values. Therefore, as you navigate this exciting phase of life, it's paramount to prioritize friendships that enrich your existence and drive you toward success.

Initiating a conversation serves as your initial stride toward establishing these meaningful connections. The art of conversation serves as the foundation of any strong friendship. It grants you the opportunity to express yourself, share your interests, opinions, and life experiences, while also gaining insight into the person across from you. These exchanges lay the groundwork for trust and respect, both vital elements in fostering a healthy friendship. Thus, present yourself as friendly, approachable, and respectful. Exhibit curiosity, attentiveness, and responsiveness. Utilize open-ended questions, compliments, humor, and shared interests to initiate and sustain engaging conversations.

Now, let's delve into expanding your social circles. An excellent approach to achieve this is by participating in clubs or organizations that resonate with your interests or aspirations. These platforms introduce you to individuals who share your passions, providing opportunities to partake in meaningful activities, acquire new skills, and contribute to your community. To identify the right club or organization for you, conduct thorough research about the offerings on your campus, attend events that align with your interests, and engage actively.

Furthermore, it's vital to remember that the friendships you have already established hold immense value. Nurturing these existing bonds is just as significant as forging new ones. Built upon mutual understanding and care, these connections bring depth and richness to your social landscape, rendering them stronger and more gratifying. Staying in touch, displaying genuine interest in your friends' lives, expressing gratitude, and celebrating their achievements are all ways to deepen these connections and make them more meaningful.

The Joys of Diversity

College is a tapestry woven with the vibrant threads of cultures, identities, and perspectives, each contributing to a colorful mosaic of diversity. This richness is not merely decorative; it serves as a dynamic force, enhancing your education and shaping you into a well-rounded individual prepared to navigate a multicultural world. However, the presence of diversity alone does not guarantee a fruitful environment. In this context, cultivating diverse friendships and nurturing an atmosphere of respect and inclusivity among your peers can yield numerous benefits for your personal and social development.

One remarkable advantage of diverse friendships is their ability to ignite creativity. As you immerse yourself in the myriad colors of these relationships, your mind becomes a fertile ground for fresh ideas, intriguing insights, and enriching experiences. It's a mental gym where your imagination receives a vigorous workout, fostering curiosity and innovation. Embracing diversity encourages you to engage with different viewpoints and critically evaluate evidence, transforming you into an intellectually flexible individual equipped with the skills demanded by modern careers and academic success.

Maintaining a diverse circle of friends also functions as a cross-cultural workshop, honing your ability to interact with individuals from various cultural backgrounds. This engagement allows you to delve into the fascinating realms of diverse cultures, languages, values, and beliefs, all while offering glimpses of your own cultural tapestry. These interactions dispel stereotypes, prejudices, and biases, replacing them with empathy, respect, and a profound appreciation for cultural diversity. The outcome is your emergence as a global citizen, characterized by tolerance, open-mindedness, and inclusivity.

Another invaluable aspect of these friendships is personal growth. As you reflect on both your commonalities and distinctions with your friends, you gain a deeper understanding of yourself, your strengths, and your values. Willingness to venture into uncharted territory leads to an expansion of your comfort zone, a reassessment of your assumptions, and the acquisition of skills to navigate ambiguity.

To truly experience the magic of diversity, you must foster an environment of respect and inclusivity. It involves creating a space where everyone feels at home, regardless of their background, culture, identity, or perspective. Picture it as orchestrating the diverse musical notes into a harmonious symphony, where each unique sound is cherished and celebrated. Here are some practical steps to achieve this:

- Explore your own cultural identity and biases while appreciating the diversity around you.
- Display genuine curiosity and a willingness to learn from those who differ from you.
- Exhibit consideration in all your interactions.
- Promote collaboration and mutual support in your activities.
- Be open to adjusting your attitudes and opinions.
- Let empathy and compassion guide your feelings and actions towards others.

By embracing these principles, you can create a thriving environment that not only celebrates diversity but also cultivates a profound sense of unity and understanding among all its members.

Standing Up for Yourself

Let's talk about assertive communication—a skill that can truly be a game-changer for your college journey. It's all about finding that sweet spot between respect and straightforwardness, allowing you to express your needs and feelings in a clear and considerate manner. This skill will not only enhance your relationships but also sharpen your communication abilities, ultimately propelling you closer to your academic and personal goals.

Picture this: you're engaged in a lively discussion with your peers, tackling various topics and sharing your viewpoints. Now, speaking up confidently in such situations can be a bit daunting, especially when your thoughts differ from the popular consensus or face resistance. But fear not, because here are some strategies to help you ace it:

- Embrace the "I" perspective. Instead of saying, "You're incorrect," try something like, "I see it differently." This small shift keeps the conversation centered around your ideas, avoiding the potential pitfalls of blame games or heated arguments.
- Build your arguments on facts. Swap out "This is terrible" with "This idea seems to have a few pitfalls..." By grounding your thoughts in solid reasoning, you maintain objectivity and avoid biased judgments.
- Cultivate respect. Even in the midst of a passionate discussion, it's important to prevent it from turning into a battle. Instead of dismissing an opposing view as "ridiculous," consider responding with, "That's a novel viewpoint; could you elaborate?" This approach fosters respect and keeps the door open for constructive dialogue.

With these assertive communication techniques in your tool-box, you'll be better equipped to navigate discussions, express your ideas confidently, and engage with your peers in a way that promotes mutual respect and understanding. So, go ahead and give it a try—it's a valuable skill that will serve you well throughout your college journey and beyond!

Roommate 101

Navigating Nudity with Roommates

Living with roommates often involves encountering their habits and preferences, including their comfort levels with nudity. While some individuals may feel at ease with nudity, others may find it uncomfortable or inappropriate. Addressing this situation effectively is essential for maintaining a respectful and tension-free living environment.

Practical Solutions:

Initiating an Honest Conversation

Initiating an Honest Conversation: Start by having an open and straightforward talk about the issue. Choose a time when you and your roommates can sit down and chat. Use relatable language and express your feelings honestly. For instance, say, "Hey, I've got to be real with you – seeing someone in the buff in our shared living room makes me pretty uncomfortable."

Encourage Open Dialogue

Encourage Your Roommates to Share: After you've shared your feelings, encourage your roommates to do the same.

Make them feel comfortable discussing their comfort levels and boundaries regarding nudity. Show that you're willing to listen and understand where they're coming from.

Establish Clear Rules Together

Create Clear Rules Together: If needed, work together to create some simple and agreed-upon rules regarding nudity in common areas. These rules should respect everyone's comfort zones. You might say something like, "Can we all agree not to go au naturel in the living room? It'd make things a lot less awkward for everyone."

Define Private Spaces

Define Private Spaces: If you share a space, make sure to define which areas are considered "private" and "shared." Clearly mark where nudity is off-limits, so everyone knows where personal privacy is respected.

Show Mutual Respect

Respect Each Other: Once you've set up some ground rules, be sure to follow them. Show that you respect your room-mates' boundaries and expect the same in return. A little respect can go a long way in making sure everyone feels comfortable at home.

By following these practical steps and having an open conversation in a relatable manner, you can address the issue of nudity with your roommates more effectively and promote mutual understanding and a peaceful living situation.

LGBTQ Roommates

Living with LGBTQ roommates can be a rewarding experience that offers the opportunity to learn, grow, and build meaningful relationships. To ensure a harmonious living situation and promote inclusivity, consider the following strategies:

Practical Solutions:

Educate Yourself about LGBTQ Experiences

Creating a safe and inclusive living environment starts with educating yourself about LGBTQ experiences, challenges, and identities. Make an effort to understand the terminology and correct usage of pronouns to ensure that you're respectful and sensitive in your interactions with LGBTQ roommates.

Initiate Open and Non-Judgmental Conversations

Initiate open and non-judgmental conversations about LGBTQ topics. Encourage your roommates to share their experiences, concerns, and perspectives. Be a good listener and express genuine interest in learning from them. By fostering a culture of respect and acceptance, you can create an environment where everyone feels valued and understood.

Avoid Making Assumptions

Avoid making assumptions about your LGBTQ roommates' experiences or identities. Instead, ask questions and seek clarification when needed. Understanding that everyone's journey is unique and that you may not fully grasp their experiences can help prevent conflicts and promote mutual respect.

Approach Conflicts with Patience and Empathy

In cases where conflicts or misunderstandings do arise, approach the situation with patience and empathy. Open dialogue is key to resolving conflicts related to LGBTQ issues. Remember that your LGBTQ roommates are individuals with their own stories and emotions, and it's important to treat them with the same respect and consideration you would expect in return.

By actively engaging with your LGBTQ roommates, educating yourself, and maintaining open communication, you can foster a supportive and harmonious living environment that values diversity and inclusivity.

Religious/Spiritual Issues

Religious and spiritual beliefs are deeply personal and can vary widely among individuals. When roommates with different belief systems come together, conflicts may arise over various aspects such as dietary requirements, decorations, daily rituals, and more. It's essential to navigate these differences with respect and understanding.

Practical Solutions:

Respect for Beliefs

Respect is the cornerstone of resolving conflicts related to religious or spiritual differences. Begin by acknowledging and respecting your roommates' beliefs, just as you expect them to respect yours. Understand that diversity in religious and spiritual practices is a part of a multicultural and inclusive living environment.

Open and Honest Communication

Initiate open and honest conversations about religious and spiritual practices. Share your own beliefs and practices while actively listening to your roommates' perspectives. This dialogue can help you gain insight into each other's values and needs.

Willingness to Compromise

In situations where conflicts arise, be willing to compromise. Find common ground that allows everyone to coexist peacefully. For example, if you have different dietary requirements due to religious beliefs, discuss how to store and prepare food in a way that accommodates both sets of dietary restrictions.

Creating Shared Spaces

Designate shared spaces where religious or spiritual practices can be performed without infringing on anyone else's comfort. This could include setting up a designated meditation area or prayer space within your living quarters.

Celebrating Diversity

Embrace the opportunity to learn about different religious and spiritual traditions. Participate in celebrations or ceremonies, if invited, to show your support and understanding.

Conflict Resolution

If conflicts related to religious or spiritual issues do arise, approach them with empathy and a willingness to find solutions that respect everyone's beliefs. Seeking the assistance of a mediator or residence advisor may be helpful in resolving complex conflicts.

By prioritizing respect, open communication, compromise, and inclusivity, you can navigate religious and spiritual differences with your roommates while maintaining a harmonious living environment that values diversity.

Sex, Masturbation, and Roommate Liaisons

Living in shared spaces may occasionally involve conflicts related to sexual activity, masturbation, or roommate liaisons. These situations can be sensitive and may lead to discomfort or tension if not addressed properly.

Practical Solutions:

Privacy Needs and Boundaries

Open and honest communication about privacy needs and boundaries is essential. Initiate a conversation with your roommates to discuss your expectations and preferences regarding privacy, especially in shared living areas. Encourage your roommates to do the same.

Establish Clear Ground Rules

If you have specific rules or expectations regarding sexual activity or masturbation, discuss and agree upon them with your roommates. Having clear, mutually agreed-upon ground rules can help prevent misunderstandings and conflicts.

Shared Spaces vs. Private Spaces

Distinguish between shared and private spaces within your living quarters. Clarify which areas are designated for personal privacy and which areas should be kept free from sexual activity.

Respect for Shared Spaces

Maintain respect for shared spaces by ensuring they remain clean and suitable for all roommates. If a sexual encounter occurs, ensure that it's conducted discreetly and in accordance with any established ground rules.

Open and Non-judgmental Communication

Encourage an environment where roommates can openly discuss their needs and concerns related to sexual activity. Avoid making assumptions about your roommates' preferences and comfort levels.

Conflict Resolution

In the event of a conflict or discomfort related to sexual activity, address the issue calmly and respectfully. Seek mutually agreeable solutions that prioritize everyone's comfort and privacy.

By fostering open communication, setting clear boundaries, and respecting each other's privacy needs, you can navigate issues related to sexual activity, masturbation, and roommate liaisons more effectively and maintain a harmonious living environment.

Building Trust and Addressing Lying/Stealing Issues with Roommates

Trust is the bedrock of any successful roommate relationship. However, when trust is violated through dishonesty, such as lying or stealing, it can lead to significant conflicts and a toxic living environment. To address these issues effectively, consider implementing practical solutions that promote trust, resolution, and harmonious cohabitation.

Practical Solutions:

Honest Conversations

Initiating an Honest Conversation: Begin by having open and honest conversations with your roommates. Choose a time when everyone can sit down and talk. Use straightforward and relatable language to express your feelings honestly. For example, you could say, "Hey, I need to be upfront with you – I've noticed some of my things have gone missing, and it's making me uneasy."

Encourage Accountability

Encourage your roommates to take responsibility for their actions. If one of them admits to lying or stealing, it's vital to discuss the consequences and express how it has affected you and the overall living situation. Fostering accountability can be a critical step in rebuilding trust.

Seek Mediation

When open communication alone doesn't resolve the issue, seeking mediation can be a sensible approach. A neutral third party, such as a mediator or counselor, can facilitate a constructive dialogue between roommates. Mediation provides a structured and safe environment for discussing concerns and working towards solutions.

Establish Boundaries and Agreements

To prevent future conflicts related to trust, consider creating clear boundaries and agreements with your roommates.

These agreements should include guidelines on respecting each other's privacy, property, and personal space. Put these boundaries in writing and ensure that all roommates agree and sign the document. This can serve as a reference point in case of future disagreements.

Promote Accountability and Transparency

Encourage a culture of accountability and transparency within your living space. Roommates should feel comfortable discussing their actions, concerns, and expectations openly. Regular check-ins or house meetings can be an effective way to maintain clear communication and ensure that everyone is on the same page.

Seek Professional Assistance

In cases where trust issues persist and negatively impact your living situation, consider seeking professional assistance. A counselor or therapist can help roommates address underlying issues contributing to the breach of trust and develop strategies for rebuilding a healthy living environment.

By implementing these practical solutions and focusing on open communication, accountability, and conflict resolution, you can work towards rebuilding trust with your roommates and maintaining a harmonious living environment. Trust is a vital component of roommate relationships, and addressing trust issues directly can lead to a healthier and more positive shared living experience.

Drunk or High Roommates

Living with roommates can bring together individuals with diverse views on substance use. While some may have no issue with it, others may find frequent intoxication disruptive or concerning. To maintain a harmonious household, it's crucial to address these differences in a respectful and proactive manner.

Practical Solutions:

Open and Honest Dialogue

Initiating an Honest Conversation: Begin by having an open and honest conversation with your roommates about substance use. Choose a time when everyone can engage in a calm and non-judgmental discussion. Use "I" statements to express your concerns and feelings. For instance, you might say, "I've noticed that frequent intoxication in our shared spaces affects my ability to focus on my responsibilities and makes me uncomfortable."

Establish Clear Boundaries

Work together to establish clear and mutually agreed-upon boundaries regarding substance use within shared spaces. Determine which areas are designated as "private" and where substance use is permitted or prohibited. Having written guidelines can help ensure that everyone's comfort zones are respected. You might agree, for example, that substance use is limited to individual bedrooms or specific common areas.

Promote Responsible Use

Encourage roommates who choose to engage in substance use to do so responsibly and respectfully. Emphasize the importance of moderation, safety, and consideration for others in shared living spaces. Encourage open dialogue about responsible substance use, and discuss the potential impacts on individual and collective responsibilities within the household.

Create a Schedule or Agreement

Consider creating a schedule or agreement for substance use within shared spaces. This can help ensure that intoxication doesn't interfere with roommate responsibilities, such as chores, study time, or shared activities. A schedule might include designated "quiet hours" during which substance use is discouraged to maintain a peaceful environment.

Express Concerns Calmly

If you have concerns about your roommates' substance use, address them calmly and respectfully. Avoid judgment or accusations. Instead, express your feelings and observations using "I" statements. For example, you could say, "I've noticed that when there's frequent intoxication in our shared spaces, it can lead to disruptions, and I'm concerned about our household's overall well-being."

Seek Mediation if Necessary

In cases where conflicts or misunderstandings persist, consider seeking mediation. A neutral third party, such as a counselor or mediator, can facilitate a constructive dialogue between roommates. Mediation provides a structured and unbiased platform for discussing concerns, finding compromises, and reaching agreements that support a peaceful living environment.

By implementing these practical solutions and emphasizing open communication, responsible behavior, and conflict resolution, you can navigate differences in substance use with your roommates more effectively. Creating a household where everyone's comfort, responsibilities, and concerns are respected is essential for maintaining a peaceful and harmonious living environment.

Messy Roommates

Differing standards of cleanliness among roommates can potentially result in conflicts and resentment. Addressing this issue effectively is vital for ensuring a harmonious living environment.

Practical Solutions:

Create a Cleaning Schedule

One practical approach to mitigate conflicts related to cleanliness is to create a cleaning schedule. Sit down with your roommates and allocate specific cleaning duties to each person. Establish a regular cleaning routine that includes tasks such as vacuuming, dusting, and bathroom cleaning. Make sure everyone is aware of their responsibilities and the schedule for completing them.

Divide Chores Equitably

When dividing cleaning chores, aim for equity. Consider each person's schedule, availability, and preferences when assigning tasks. Rotate responsibilities regularly to ensure that no one feels burdened or unfairly treated. For example, you can agree to switch chores every week or month to distribute the workload evenly.

Establish Clear Expectations

Communicate openly with your roommates about your expectations regarding cleanliness. Share your standards and preferences for a clean living space, and encourage your roommates to do the same. By understanding each other's perspectives, you can work towards a compromise that respects everyone's comfort levels.

Address Issues Promptly

If cleanliness issues arise, address them promptly but diplomatically. Avoid confrontations or accusations and instead opt for a calm and respectful conversation. Use "I" statements to express your concerns and feelings. For instance, you might say, "I've noticed that the kitchen hasn't been as clean as we agreed, and it's important to me that we all contribute to keeping our shared spaces tidy."

Accountability Check-Ins

Implement regular accountability check-ins with your roommates to assess the cleanliness of your shared spaces. During these check-ins, discuss whether everyone is fulfilling their cleaning duties and whether adjustments to the cleaning schedule or responsibilities are necessary. This practice helps maintain transparency and ensures that cleanliness remains a shared priority.

Celebrate Achievements

Recognize and celebrate achievements in maintaining a clean living space. Express appreciation for your roommates' contributions to cleanliness, and acknowledge when improvements have been made. Positive reinforcement can motivate everyone to continue working together to keep your shared areas tidy.

By applying these practical solutions and fostering open communication, equitable chore distribution, and a shared commitment to cleanliness, you can effectively address conflicts arising from differing cleanliness standards among roommates. Creating a clean and harmonious living environment that respects everyone's preferences and responsibilities is key to a peaceful cohabitation.

Chatty/Noisy Roommates

Diverse social needs among roommates can lead to conflicts, especially when one roommate prefers peace and quiet while the other tends to be chatty or noisy. Addressing this situation requires effective communication and compromise.

Practical Solutions:

Define Quiet Hours

To create a harmonious living environment, consider defining specific quiet hours during which noise should be minimized. Collaboratively decide on a reasonable time-frame for these quiet hours that accommodates everyone's needs. For instance, you can agree on quiet hours from 10:00 PM to 7:00 AM to ensure that everyone has an opportunity for uninterrupted rest.

Designate Quiet Zones

Designate specific areas within your living space as "quiet zones." For example, you can declare the living room or study area as a quiet zone where noise should be kept to a minimum. This allows roommates who require quiet to have dedicated spaces for solitude while still permitting social interaction in other areas.

Communicate Your Needs

Encourage open and honest communication about your social needs and preferences with your roommates. Express your desire for quiet or your need for social interaction calmly and respectfully. For instance, you can say, "I appreciate our conversations, but there are times when I need quiet to study or unwind."

Active Listening and Empathy

Practice active listening when your roommates express their social needs. Understand that everyone has different preferences, and it's essential to empathize with their perspectives. Engage in a constructive dialogue to find common ground that respects each other's requirements for social interaction and solitude.

Collaborate on Schedules

Collaboratively create schedules that accommodate both quiet and social hours. Negotiate specific times when you can expect some noise and other times when you can enjoy peace and quiet. This compromise ensures that everyone's needs are considered.

Utilize Noise-Canceling Options

For moments when noise is unavoidable, consider using noise-canceling headphones or white noise machines. These tools can help mitigate disturbances and provide you with the quiet atmosphere you need, even when your roommates are engaged in social activities.

By applying these practical solutions, which include establishing quiet hours, designating quiet zones, openly discussing social needs, and finding a balance through collaboration and compromise, you can effectively address conflicts related to chatty or noisy roommates. Creating an environment that respects varying social preferences while maintaining open communication is key to harmonious cohabitation.

Math, Mind, and Mentor: Olivia's Triumph

Unlike your typical math student, let's meet Olivia – a vibrant whirlwind of color and unpredictability. She had this incredible knack for finding beauty in numbers, patterns, and equations, sensing an enchanting harmony that connected everything from teeny-tiny particles to those faraway twinkling stars. But in this intricate mathematical waltz, she stumbled more than a few times. Math was like a captivating language she adored but didn't always grasp completely. Her curious mind wandered off, making it a tad challenging to keep up with her studies. The once-enticing world of math was slowly losing its charm, replaced by the icy clutches of self-doubt and fear.

Now, picture Professor Graham, the kind of teacher who could turn even the most baffling concepts into something as understandable as your favorite song lyrics. His students loved him not just for his genius but also for his down-to-earth warmth and humility.

Fast forward to Olivia's sophomore year, and she's suddenly hit with the cold, hard reality of failing grades and thoughts of giving up on her dream. The subject she once adored felt like an insurmountable mountain. But then, there was Professor Graham, noticing her stumbles and inviting her to his office one day. He sat there, listening, offering a comforting silence that somehow understood all of her struggles. And then he said, "Olivia, your passion for math shines through your eyes. But remember, we all have our unique rhythms. Your struggle isn't a failure; it's a testament to your courage in tackling something challenging."

He made her a promise – to break down those thorny concepts, to help her focus, and to reveal the creative spark within her. With his unwavering support, Olivia began to regain her footing. They spent countless hours together, brainstorming ideas, solving problems, and even delving into cosmic discussions about the universe's beauty and order. Olivia embraced Professor Graham's guidance and found a special connection with his focusing techniques. Sure, there were still those tough days when her old insecurities tried to creep back in. But now, she had a guiding light, someone reminding her that it's perfectly normal to struggle. Her academic journey was no straight path; it was a winding trail filled with ups and downs.

As she wrapped up her studies, Olivia had transformed into a confident math major, a person brimming with newfound resilience and a deep understanding of her abilities. She owed this transformation to Professor Graham, the mentor who had not only taught her to decode numbers but also helped her embrace her unique learning style.

Olivia's story illustrates the power of mentorship, turning struggles into strengths. It emphasizes the importance of compassion and understanding in the world of learning. Students are not empty vessels; they are brilliant minds waiting to be inspired and nurtured. If you find yourself facing similar academic challenges, remember Olivia's journey. Seek guidance, reach out to mentors or professors, and don't hesitate to ask for help. Embrace your unique learning style, and understand that difficulties are part of the learning process. With the right support and determination, you can transform your struggles into strengths, just like Olivia did.

College, with its blend of rigorous academics and personal growth, can challenge even the most independent souls. The next chapter will dive into the crucial skills you'll need to thrive, not just academically, but emotionally, mentally, and physically. Get ready to embark on this transformative journey!

Key Takeaways

- **Embrace Common Feelings:** It's normal to feel anxious and isolated when starting college, but remember, you're not alone—many students share these emotions.
- **Seek Connection:** Whether you're an introvert or extrovert, you can find connections through shared interests and mutual efforts. College is a place to form meaningful relationships.
- **Balance Solitude:** While solitude can be comforting, don't let it become isolating. Striking a balance between personal time and social

engagement is crucial for a fulfilling college experience.

- **Explore Opportunities:** College offers a wide range of group activities and hobbies. Don't hesitate to try new things, from sports to drama, to discover your passions and make friends who share your interests. College is a journey of self-discovery and connection —embrace it!

5 NAVIGATING COLLEGE WITH SPECIAL EDUCATION NEEDS

Embracing a New Chapter in Education

As you step into the exciting world of college, ready to embrace new experiences and broaden your horizons, it's essential to acknowledge that this transition may present unique challenges, particularly if you've navigated high school with special education needs. But the good news is, college can be a time of remarkable growth, empowerment, and achievement for you. This chapter is your guide to arming yourself with the tools, knowledge, and confidence to make your college journey not only successful but also incredibly fulfilling.

In high school, you may have benefited from a tailored support system that addressed your special education needs, including Individualized Education Programs (IEPs) and educators who understood your distinct learning style. As you venture into the college environment, which brings fresh experiences and a different approach to learning, it's natural to feel a bit overwhelmed initially. However, this transition also opens up a world of opportunities for further personal development, exploration of new interests, and the creation of a life that aligns with your dreams and capabilities.

College isn't just about academics; it's a voyage of self-discovery. As a student with special education needs, you'll become adept at advocating for yourself in ways you might not have explored before. You'll uncover your strengths, learn how to overcome challenges with resilience, and develop the determination to thrive.

In the pages that follow, we'll delve into understanding your rights as a college student with special education needs, getting ready for the transition, discovering and utilizing campus resources, and much more. Our aim is to equip you with the knowledge and strategies necessary to not only succeed but also excel in college, ensuring that your educational journey is both triumphant and enriching.

Always keep in mind that your college journey is uniquely yours. With the right resources and a proactive approach, you're not just destined to succeed; you're primed to shine.

Understanding Your Rights

Entering college means entering a new world of rights and responsibilities, especially for students with special education needs. It's crucial to understand that while college provides different protections than high school, you still have rights. Key among these are the Americans with Disabilities Act (ADA) and Section 504 of the Rehabilitation Act. These laws ensure that you have equal access to education and the right to reasonable accommodations for your learning needs.

The transition from high school to college is significant in terms of how these laws apply. In high school, under the Individuals with Disabilities Education Act (IDEA), you might have had an IEP that outlined specific services and support. In college, IDEA no longer applies, but the ADA and Section 504 do. This means that while colleges are required to provide accommodations, they are not required to identify you or design specialized programs. It's more about providing access and leveling the playing field.

This shift calls for a more proactive role in your education. You'll need to self-identify to your college's disability services office and possibly provide documentation of your disability. Remember, this is about ensuring that you receive the support you need, not about labeling you. It's a step toward independence and self-advocacy – key skills in college and beyond.

Preparing for the Transition

The move from high school to college is not just a physical one; it's a transition in mindset and approach. For students with special education needs, preparation is key. Start by understanding your learning style and the accommodations that have worked for you in the past. Self-awareness is a powerful tool in college.

Next, it's time to develop your self-advocacy skills. In college, you are your own best advocate. This means understanding your rights, knowing what accommodations you need, and being able to communicate these needs effectively to the right people. Practice expressing your needs clearly and confidently.

Also, consider creating an updated plan similar to your high school IEP for your personal use. While colleges don't follow IEPs, having a plan can help you articulate your needs and goals. This plan might include your learning strategies, potential accommodations, and who to contact for support.

Before the semester starts, reach out to your college's disability services office. They can guide you on the process of registering for accommodations, what documentation you'll need, and other services they offer. This is also a great time to connect with any student support groups or services that can aid your transition.

Remember, preparation for college is not just about academic readiness; it's also about being ready to take charge of your education and your needs. The more prepared you are, the smoother your transition to college will be.

Identifying College Resources

Once you're familiar with your rights and have begun preparing for the transition, the next step is to identify the resources available to you in college. Most colleges have a disability support services office (sometimes known by different names), which is your primary resource. This office can provide accommodations like note-taking services, extended time for exams, alternative exam locations, and assistive technology. They can also help you navigate the college environment, academically and socially.

But don't stop there. Explore other campus resources that can enhance your college experience. Libraries often have resources for students with learning differences, counseling centers can offer support for emotional challenges, and career services can assist with internships and job place-ments post-graduation. Remember, these services are there to help you succeed.

- **Document Instances:** Keep detailed records of instances when your accommodations are not met, including dates, specific classes, and descriptions of the situation. This can be important if you need to escalate the matter.
- **Re-Communicate with Disability Services:** If direct communication with the professor does not resolve the issue, revisit your college's disability support services. They can intervene and help clarify the

accommodations with your professor or the department.

- **Formal Grievance Procedure:** Most colleges have a formal grievance procedure for students to follow if their needs are not being met. If necessary, file a formal complaint. Your disability services office can guide you on how to proceed with this process.
- **Seek Support from Campus Advocacy Groups:** Many colleges have student advocacy groups or an ombudsman who can offer assistance and advice in resolving such issues. They can provide additional support and guidance on how to navigate these challenges.
- **Legal Action as a Last Resort:** If your accommodations are still not being met and you believe your rights under the ADA or Section 504 are being violated, consider seeking legal advice. Legal action is generally a last resort and should be pursued only after exhausting other avenues.

Remember, it's important to advocate for yourself and ensure that your educational needs are met. Your college is legally obligated to provide these

accommodations, and there are systems in place to support you in this process. Stay proactive, informed, and assertive about your needs, and don't hesitate to use the resources available to you for support and guidance.

Academic Support Services

Colleges typically offer academic support services that can be especially beneficial for students with special education needs. These services may include:

- **Disability Services Office:** Most colleges have a disability services office or a similar department. Contact this office as soon as possible to:
- Register your special education needs.
- Discuss and request accommodations tailored to your specific requirements, such as extended test-taking time, note-taking assistance, or accessible learning materials.
- Understand the documentation needed to verify your disability and eligibility for accommodations.
- **Academic Advising:** Your college's academic advising office can provide guidance on course selection, degree planning, and academic requirements. They can also help you align your academic goals with your individual learning needs.
- **Tutoring and Learning Centers:** Many colleges offer tutoring and learning centers that provide academic support. These centers can help you with coursework, study skills, and strategies for academic success.
- **Accessible Learning Materials:** Inquire about accessible learning materials, such as textbooks in alternative formats (e.g., audiobooks, digital texts, or

Braille) through your college's library or disability services office.

- **Mental Health and Counseling Services:** College life can be stressful, and it's essential to prioritize your mental health. Utilize on-campus counseling services to address emotional challenges and stress management.
- **Assistive Technology Labs:** Some colleges have assistive technology labs equipped with specialized software and hardware to assist students with disabilities. Explore these resources for assistive technologies that can aid in your studies.
- **Peer Mentorship Programs:** Check if your college offers peer mentorship programs. Connecting with a mentor who has experience navigating college with special education needs can provide valuable guidance and support.
- **Career Services:** As you progress through college, career services can assist you in exploring career options, building resumes, and preparing for job interviews, ensuring a smooth transition to the workforce.
- **Financial Aid Office:** Seek information on financial aid options and scholarships specifically designed for students with disabilities. These resources can help alleviate the financial burden of college.
- **Online Resources and Support Groups:** Explore online communities and support groups that cater to college students with special education needs.

These platforms can provide a sense of camaraderie and valuable advice.

- **Advocacy Groups:** Look for local or national advocacy groups that focus on the rights and support of students with disabilities. These organizations often offer resources and guidance on navigating college.
- **Campus Accessibility:** Familiarize yourself with the campus layout and accessibility features, such as accessible entrances, ramps, and designated parking spaces for students with disabilities.
- **Time Management Workshops:** Consider attending time management and study skills workshops offered by your college to improve your organizational and time management skills.

Key Takeaways

- **College Offers Growth and Success:** College is an opportunity for incredible personal growth, empowerment, and success, even if you've navigated high school with special education needs. Approach this new chapter with a positive outlook, knowing that you have the potential to thrive.
- **Understanding Your Rights:** While the transition from high school to college involves changes in how your rights are protected, remember that the Americans with Disabilities Act (ADA) and Section 504 of the Rehabilitation Act still ensure equal

access to education and reasonable accommodations.

- **Preparation and Self-Advocacy:** Prepare for the transition by understanding your learning style, developing self-advocacy skills, and creating a personalized plan that articulates your needs and goals. College requires a proactive approach to education and self-advocacy.

- **Identifying Resources:** Recognize the importance of identifying and utilizing college resources. Disability support services, academic advising, tutoring centers, counseling services, assistive technology labs, and more are available to help you succeed academically and personally.

- **Advocating for Your Needs:** Understand that advocating for your needs is essential. Keep records of any instances where your accommodations aren't met, communicate with professors and disability support services, and seek support from campus advocacy groups or legal action if necessary. Your education and rights matter, and there are avenues to ensure they are respected and upheld.

6 STRONGER, BETTER, FASTER

Strength does not come from winning. Your struggles develop your strengths. That is strength when you go through hardships and decide not to surrender. –Arnold Schwarzenegger

I n this chapter, you'll delve into actionable strategies aimed at cultivating mental serenity. These approaches will empower you to effectively cope with stress and anxiety, bolster your resilience, nurture a sense of independence and responsibility, and embrace mindful self-care routines. The ultimate aim is to assist you in crafting a well-rounded and satisfying student life.

Why Is College So Emotionally Challenging?

College is a step up from high school, presenting more substantial and diverse academic demands. Here, you're not just a student; you're the captain of your educational voyage. The pressure to navigate these challenging waters brews a potent stress cocktail, often leading to overwhelming anxiety and depression.

A Fear That Looms Large

The fear of failure extends beyond academics and permeates your broader college experience. It's a phase where you're sculpting your identity and making life-altering decisions. The weight of societal, familial, and self-imposed expectations can fuel a constant sense of stress and anxiety. The fear of making wrong choices and falling short of those expectations can be suffocating.

Navigating the Social Maze

Building new friendships, assimilating into social circles, and nurturing relationships can be emotionally taxing. For many, bonding with others isn't effortless, resulting in feelings of isolation and loneliness. Leaving behind the familiar faces of home further intensifies this sense of solitude. College often marks the first step into independent life, making the absence of a familiar support system palpable. The transition from adolescence to adulthood involves continual change, testing your resilience in a whirlwind of new environments and responsibilities.

The Weight of Financial Stress

The towering costs of tuition, accommodation, textbooks, and daily expenses can trigger financial anxiety. Many students opt for part-time jobs, adding to an already substantial workload. Balancing work and studies can blur your focus, hindering both academic and personal growth.

The Neglected Basics

Neglecting rest, maintaining an unbalanced diet, shunning exercise, and indulging in unhealthy habits like excessive alcohol consumption can wreak havoc on your physical and emotional well-being. These often-overlooked factors can significantly contribute to feelings of anxiety and depression.

The Digital Dilemma

While technology connects us, the burden of maintaining an online presence can add to your troubles. Social media can act as a double-edged sword, fueling feelings of inadequacy and loneliness when comparing your life to curated narratives. The pressure to project a picture-perfect life online can lead to a disconcerting disconnect from reality, intensifying emotional distress.

Guiding Light of Assistance

Amid these challenges, educational institutions play a crucial role. They must acknowledge the storms you face and provide support through counseling, stress management workshops, and fostering a supportive community. By promoting a balanced approach to work and life, they pave the way for a nurturing environment conducive to both academic and personal growth.

Navigating the Emotional Storm

Emotional challenges in college are complex and inter-twined. Academic pressures, social dynamics, personal development, fear of failure, financial burdens, health concerns, and the digital landscape together create a challenging backdrop that can lead to anxiety, depression, and loneliness. Yet, with guidance from educational institutions, friends, and family, you can overcome these obstacles and make the most of this invaluable phase of life. Acknowledging and addressing these emotional challenges is key to emerging as confident, resilient, and emotionally healthy individuals.

Reframing Negative or Unhelpful Thoughts

In the grand theater of life, it's not uncommon to find yourself caught in the gusts of harmful self-talk – those subtle whispers that cast shadows on your spirit, sow seeds of self-doubt, and shackle your boundless potential. These thoughts create a canvas of despair, echoing phrases like "Can I really handle this test?" "Do I fit in here, or am I like the odd one out?" or "Have I turned into an expert at messing things up (and not the fun kind)?" Yet, these are nothing more than treacherous illusions woven from distortions, exaggerations, or unfounded assumptions, devoid of a solid footing in facts or evidence.

- In this chapter, we're diving into a journey that can change the way you think. You'll discover how to recognize, understand, and turn those harmful thoughts into positive ones that can make your life better. This shift in perspective can help reduce stress, anxiety, and sadness, boost your self-confidence, ignite your motivation, and bring more happiness into your life.

- You might be wondering how to start this process. Well, we've got a bunch of steps and strategies to help you out. As we go through this chapter, we'll reveal the secrets of becoming a master at turning negative or unhelpful thoughts into something better. So, get ready to upgrade your mental toolbox and join us on this enlightening adventure!

Cultivate Thought Awareness

Foster Thought Awareness: Your initial objective is to develop the skill of recognizing these detrimental whispers and understanding their origins. Utilize mindfulness techniques to observe your thoughts, emotions, and sensations in the present moment without judgment. This practice enables you to delve into your thought patterns and their impact on your well-being. Alternatively, maintaining a journal or notebook can help externalize your thoughts, providing you with a more objective view of your inner world.

By consistently engaging in these practices, you'll gain deeper insights into your thought processes, recognizing recurring patterns and triggers that lead to unhelpful or negative thinking. Moreover, you'll uncover the connection between your thoughts and your emotional state, offering valuable information to reshape your perspective.

Keep in mind that cultivating thought awareness is a gradual process. Patience is key as you allow the practice to unfold naturally. With each step, you'll become better equipped to navigate your thoughts and transform them into tools for personal growth and mental resilience.

Subject Your Thoughts to Scrutiny

Now, let's move on to the next phase where you'll put your thoughts through a thorough examination, scrutinizing their validity and usefulness. Here's how you can approach it:

- **Question their Validity:** Begin by asking if your thought is grounded in reality. Challenge it by seeking concrete evidence to either support or refute it. This step helps you discern whether your thought is based on facts or unfounded assumptions.

- **Assess their Utility:** Evaluate whether the thought is constructive or destructive. Consider how it affects your emotions and behaviors. Does it empower you, or does it drag you down? Understanding the impact of your thoughts is crucial for reshaping your mindset.

- **Identify Cognitive Distortions:** Recognize any cognitive distortions that might be influencing your thoughts. These distortions can include magnification (making issues seem larger than they are), overgeneralization (drawing broad conclusions from limited experiences), or black-and-white thinking (seeing things as all good or all bad).

- **Examine Consequences:** Think about the potential consequences of embracing this thought. How might it impact your decisions, relationships, or well-being? Understanding the potential fallout can motivate you to adopt a more constructive perspective.

By subjecting your thoughts to this critical examination, you'll gain a deeper understanding of their nature and how they shape your perception of reality. This self-awareness is a crucial step towards reframing negative or unhelpful thoughts, allowing you to make conscious choices about the beliefs you hold and the impact they have on your life. Remember, this process takes time and practice, so be patient with yourself as you work towards reshaping your thought patterns.

Craft Positive Alternatives

Now, let's delve into your third mission, which is all about cultivating positive and constructive thought patterns. Here are some effective techniques to help you reshape your thoughts:

- **Socratic Questioning:** Challenge negative thoughts by asking yourself probing questions. Encourage critical thinking by inquiring about the evidence behind your thoughts, their validity, and alternative perspectives. This method helps you gain clarity and develop a more balanced view.

- **Guided Imagery:** Visualize positive outcomes and scenarios. When you catch yourself in a negative thought loop, redirect your imagination toward more optimistic possibilities. Visualization can shift your mindset and boost your confidence.

- **Positive Reframing:** Train your mind to find the silver lining in challenging situations. Instead of dwelling on the negatives, focus on the potential lessons, growth opportunities, or hidden advantages. This approach can transform setbacks into stepping stones.

- **Depersonalization:** Detach yourself from your thoughts by viewing them as passing mental events rather than absolute truths. Understand that thoughts are not facts, and they do not define your identity or worth.

- **Growth Mindset:** Embrace the belief that you can learn and grow from experiences, challenges, and failures. Cultivate a mindset that sees setbacks as opportunities for development rather than as reflections of your capabilities.

- **Positive Self-Talk:** Counteract negative thoughts with encouraging and compassionate self-talk. Replace self-criticism with self-affirmation, and remind yourself of your strengths and achievements.

By employing these techniques consistently, you can gradually shift your thought patterns towards positivity and resilience. It's important to remember that reframing negative thoughts is an ongoing process that requires practice. Be patient with yourself and celebrate your progress along the way. As you become more adept at crafting positive alternatives, you'll enhance your mental resilience and overall well-being.

Consistency Is Key

Your final task centers around the ongoing practice of this cycle—observing and reshaping your thoughts until they transform into dependable allies. Utilize reminders such as sticky notes, alarms, or dedicated apps to prompt mindfulness at various points throughout the day. Celebrate your achievements and commemorate the victories, no matter how small they may seem.

As you continue on this journey of self-transformation, you'll gradually free yourself from the clutches of harmful self-talk. Instead, you'll embark on a path of empowerment and self-discovery, fostering a mindset that bolsters your mental resilience and fuels your personal growth.

Remember that personal growth is an evolving process, and each step you take brings you closer to becoming the best version of yourself. Embrace the power of thought awareness and transformation, and watch as it unfolds in every aspect of your life, enhancing your overall well-being and resilience.

Your Biology = Your Psychology

College life can be demanding, affecting both your physical and mental well-being. To navigate this journey successfully, consider the following:

Prioritize Rest:

- Aim for 7-9 hours of quality sleep each night.
- Establish a consistent sleep schedule.
- Embrace Nourishment:
- Choose nutrient-rich meals to enhance mood and cognitive function.
- Limit fast food and sugar consumption.

Stay Active:

- Engage in physical activities you enjoy for at least 150 minutes per week.
- Cultivate Mindfulness and Stillness:
- Incorporate mindfulness practices, such as meditation or yoga, into your routine.
- Find moments of calm amid the college chaos.

Efficient Time Management:

- Create a well-structured schedule to balance academic tasks and self-care.
- Include self-care breaks within your schedule.

Embrace Your Community:

- Spend quality time with friends and family for emotional support.
- Consider study groups for collaborative learning.

Utilize Campus Resources:

- Access counseling services for emotional well-being.
- Explore fitness facilities and classes on campus.
- Make healthy food choices available on campus.

Personal Time and Enjoyment:

- Pursue hobbies and interests outside of academics.
- Practice self-reflection and journaling.

Financial Wellness:

- Create a budget and stick to it to alleviate financial stress.
- Seek financial guidance if needed.

By prioritizing these aspects, you can maintain the balance between your mental and physical health and make the most of your college experience.

Key Takeaways

- **Understanding College's Emotional Challenges:** College presents substantial academic demands, coupled with the pressure of shaping your identity and making crucial life decisions. Recognize that stress and anxiety are common, stemming from academic, social, financial, and personal pressures.
- **Recognizing Harmful Thought Patterns:** Learn to identify and challenge negative or unhelpful thoughts that can contribute to stress, anxiety, and depression. These thoughts are often distortions or exaggerations lacking factual basis.
- **Developing Thought Awareness:** Cultivate the skill of thought awareness through mindfulness techniques and journaling. This practice allows you to recognize recurring patterns and triggers that lead to unhelpful thinking.
- **Subjecting Thoughts to Scrutiny:** Examine your thoughts for validity and utility. Question whether they are based on reality, assess their impact on your emotions and behaviors, identify cognitive distortions, and evaluate potential consequences.
- **Crafting Positive Alternatives:** Implement techniques like Socratic questioning, guided imagery, positive reframing, and positive self-talk to reshape negative thoughts into constructive ones. This shift in perspective can reduce stress, boost self-confidence, and promote overall well-being.

7 WORK-SCHOOL-LIFE BALANCE

HAPPINESS IS NOT A MATTER OF INTENSITY BUT OF BALANCE, ORDER, RHYTHM, AND HARMONY. –THOMAS MERTON

Meet Brittany

Meet Brittany, a college student juggling classes, a part-time job, and helping her mom due to her health issues. Balancing everything can be overwhelming.

To stay on track, Brittany's become a scheduling pro, blocking out time for her responsibilities. She also practices quick stress-relief techniques, like meditation and short walks in the campus park.

But the pressure can still build up. After a tough exam, Brittany reached out to a college counselor who suggested she join a support group for students dealing with similar challenges.

Being part of that group made a big difference. Brittany realized it's okay to ask for help when needed. She's found her rhythm and knows that with smart planning, mindfulness, and the courage to seek assistance, she can handle college while caring for herself and her family.

The Working Student's Adventure

Now, let's introduce Liam Thompson, a bright-eyed freshman from a small coastal town who found himself navigating the overwhelming maze of university life in the big city. His dorm room resembled a cramped library, filled with books and mementos from home.

Liam worked at an old-fashioned bookstore, a treasure trove of aging paper and shelves filled with wisdom. His boss, Mr. Jennings, was kind but stern, valuing Liam's strong work ethic. Classes were a mix of excitement and stress, yet Dr. Hughes, a passionate history professor, recognized Liam's potential and fatigue. Their coffee-fueled conversations became Liam's guiding light, helping him navigate the delicate balance of work, studies, and life.

Slowly, Liam's world expanded. He made friends, explored hidden city alleys, and even dipped his toes into the world of dating. The bookstore's regular customers transformed into familiar faces, exchanging stories and wisdom.

As his grades improved, so did his quality of life. The once-daunting juggling act of work and study evolved into a well-coordinated dance. When Liam donned his graduation cap, Mr. Jennings beamed proudly from the audience. Liam's journey wasn't just about earning a degree; it was about personal growth, resilience, and the rich tapestry of connections he had woven along the way.

Balance On the Tightrope

College is a bustling marketplace brimming with opportunities to explore your passions, interests, and hobbies. Whether you join a club, engage in sports, or volunteer, these pursuits do more than just bring joy—they weave connections and enrich your college journey. Yet, amidst the vibrancy, stress often looms nearby, casting shadows of immense pressure, sleepless nights, and anxious days.

But fret not, for you possess powerful tools to shield yourself. The practices of mindfulness, positive thinking, and seeking professional guidance can serve as your protective armor. Admittedly, the path isn't always smooth. At times, you may stumble, unintentionally neglecting facets of your life due to time constraints or waning motivation. It's akin to forgetting to water a plant, which may manifest as a dip in academic performance or a dwindling sense of happiness.

Neglecting areas such as sleep or social interaction can deplete your energy, fostering feelings of isolation or unhappiness. Worse still, it may lead to a decline in mental well-being, with unhealthy coping mechanisms taking a toll on your health.

So, what's the key to navigating this intricate balancing act? It's about finding a unique equilibrium, like adjusting the sails on a boat to ensure smooth passage. Nurturing all aspects of your life is the compass that guides you to better grades, a happier heart, reduced stress, and a truly fulfilling college experience. Remember, the perfect balance isn't discovered; it's meticulously crafted with care, attention, and a deep understanding of oneself.

Avoiding Overcommitment: Finding the Right Balance

The Excitement-Overload Dilemma

Entering college as a freshman brings with it a sense of excitement and a world of opportunities. You're eager to explore new subjects, make friends, and maybe even take on a part-time job or join various extracurricular activities. While enthusiasm and a willingness to embrace new experiences are admirable qualities, it's crucial to strike a balance to avoid falling into the trap of overcommitment.

The Overcommitment Pitfall

Overcommitment occurs when you take on more responsibilities and commitments than you can realistically manage. It often stems from the desire to excel academically, build a strong resume, or simply fear of missing out on valuable experiences. However, overcommitting can lead to excessive stress, burnout, and negatively impact both your academic performance and overall well-being.

Recognizing the Signs

It's essential to recognize the signs of overcommitment early on to prevent it from taking a toll on your college experience. Here are some common indicators:

- **Feeling Overwhelmed:** If you constantly feel overwhelmed, unable to catch your breath, or find it challenging to keep up with your obligations, it's a clear sign you might be overcommitted.
- **Decline in Academic Performance:** A significant drop in your grades or difficulty in managing your coursework can be a result of spreading yourself too thin.
- **Lack of Sleep and Exhaustion:** Consistently staying up late to meet deadlines or feeling exhausted even after a full night's sleep can be indicators of overcommitment.
- **Neglecting Self-Care:** When you no longer have time for self-care activities like exercise, hobbies, or spending time with friends and family, it's a red flag.
- **Increased Irritability:** If you find yourself becoming easily irritated or losing patience with others, it might be due to the stress of overcommitment.

Strategies to Avoid Overcommitment

Now that you understand the risks of overcommitment, let's explore strategies to help you maintain a healthy balance:

- **Prioritize Your Commitments:** Identify your most important commitments, whether they are academic, work-related, or extracurricular. Focus on these and be selective about additional responsibilities.

- **Create a Schedule:** Develop a realistic daily and weekly schedule that includes dedicated time for studying, work, relaxation, and social activities.
- **Set Boundaries:** Learn to say no when necessary. It's okay to decline additional tasks or commitments if you're already stretched thin.
- **Seek Support:** Reach out to academic advisors, professors, or mentors for guidance in managing your academic workload and extracurricular activities.
- **Time Management:** Improve your time management skills by setting specific goals, breaking tasks into smaller steps, and using tools like planners or digital calendars.
- **Evaluate Your Goals:** Periodically review your goals and commitments. Consider whether they still align with your long-term objectives and make adjustments as needed.
- **Balance Self-Care:** Prioritize self-care activities, including exercise, relaxation, and spending time with loved ones. These activities help recharge your energy and reduce stress.
- **Seek Help When Needed:** If you find yourself consistently overwhelmed, don't hesitate to seek support from counseling services or student support groups on campus.

Freshman year is a time of exploration, growth, and self-discovery. While the excitement of new opportunities is thrilling, it's vital to strike a balance between your responsibilities. Recognizing the signs of overcommitment and implementing strategies to maintain a healthy balance will not only enhance your college experience but also set you on a path to personal and academic success. Remember, your journey through college is uniquely yours, and finding that perfect equilibrium is a valuable skill you'll carry with you throughout your academic and personal life.

Effective Communication: Your Ticket to Success

Welcome to the realm of academia and work, where you find yourself at a crossroads armed with your thoughts, ideas, feelings, and the words you choose to convey them. As a student managing the weight of studies and potentially a job, mastering the art of communication will be your compass through both challenges and triumphs.

Act One: Building Blocks of Communication

Communication skills are like the building blocks of a cool castle. It's all about listening, talking, writing, reading, and picking up on those nonverbal signals. Imagine being an eagle-eyed listener, a smooth-talking speaker, and a writing pro. When you master these skills, you not only boost yourself but also make things clearer for everyone around you, avoiding those awkward conflicts.

Act Two: Critical Thinking and Problem-Solving Skills

Next up, we've got critical thinking and problem-solving skills on the agenda. Picture yourself as a crafty problem solver, taking raw challenges and hammering out solutions with logic. It's all about learning to express your ideas in a convincing and creative way. When you can assess info, back up your arguments with evidence, and tailor your message for different folks, you become a super adaptable and sharp communicator.

Final Act: Open and Honest Communication

Now, let's talk about open and honest communication when it comes to your expectations and needs. Think of it as your growth garden. You're the gardener here, making sure your communication flowers and thrives with transparency and sincerity. As a student, you've got to be on top of it, chatting with your teachers, classmates, or bosses about your goals, challenges, and what you need. Don't be shy to ask for help, give some feedback, say thanks, or talk through your needs – it's like a cool breeze blowing success your way.

When the curtains close, you'll retain not just a skill but an art, a guiding force, and a companion in effective communication. You hold the palette and brushes to paint your academic and professional life with vibrant colors of understanding, collaboration, stress management, and enhanced performance. Embrace these principles and skills, and witness the world around you transform into a canvas of boundless possibilities.

Key Takeaways

- **Balancing Act:** Brittany, the college student, shows us that balancing academics, a part-time job, and family responsibilities can be overwhelming. To stay on track, Brittany excels at scheduling and practices stress-relief techniques like meditation and short walks. Seeking help when needed and joining a support group can make a big difference in managing life's challenges.

- **Liam's Journey:** Liam's story highlights a student's adventure in balancing work, life, and studies. With resilience and the support of mentors and friends, Liam navigated the challenges of university life, expanding his world along the way. His journey reminds us that personal growth and connections are integral to the college experience.

- **Balance on the Tightrope:** College life offers numerous opportunities, but it can also bring stress and pressure. Mindfulness, positive thinking, and seeking professional guidance are powerful tools to manage these challenges. Finding a unique equilibrium, nurturing all aspects of your life, and avoiding neglecting areas like sleep and social interaction are essential for a fulfilling college experience.

8 OUT OF THE NEST

T*he bond that links your true family is not one of blood but of respect and joy in each other's life.* –Richard Bach

Imagine yourself in your brand-new kitchen. It might be cozy, but it's entirely yours. The thrill of not having to rely on takeout or your parents' cooking fills you with joy. Learning to cook isn't just about satisfying your hunger; it's a symbol of independence, a delightful marker of growing up. And guess what? It can be as straightforward as mastering a favorite pasta recipe that not only saves you money but tastes exactly the way you love it.

Now, consider these life skills that extend beyond the kitchen —budgeting, cleaning, fixing a leaky faucet. While they may seem mundane, they are the stepping stones to self-sufficiency. You'll no longer have to call someone else to handle these tasks. You become the hero of your own home, conquering daily life like a pro.

But adulthood isn't solely about self-reliance; it's about building connections too. You'll need to communicate, negotiate, and sometimes even engage in disagreements. However, with the right attitude and determination, you'll form friendships, partnerships, and maybe even discover a love connection or two. It's all part of the exhilarating journey of self-discovery and understanding what you want from life. You might also embark on a new job or academic journey, further expanding your horizons. The ability to network, craft an impressive resume, or ace an interview isn't just about advancing your career; it's a means of personal growth. You're shaping your future with every email sent, hand shaken, and success celebrated.

Undoubtedly, adulting can be challenging, but it's also incredibly thrilling and fulfilling. Remember, you're not alone on this adventure. With each step, you'll uncover more of yourself and your true capabilities. Embrace the beauty of becoming an adult; it's a journey worth savoring.

The Parent Trap

Navigating the evolving dynamics with your parents is pivotal during this transitional phase. Once your primary caregivers and mentors, they now find themselves grappling with the idea of loosening the reins. This shift can sometimes lead to tension and conflicts as they struggle to let go of control, a process often marked by resistance. Why does this struggle persist? The reasons are multifaceted:

- **Invested Support:** Parents have dedicated significant time, energy, and resources to nurture your success. Their pride in your achievements coexists with anxiety about the future, along with the fear of losing the close connection and influence they've had as you venture into independence.
- **Entrenched Parenting Habits:** Habits and routines associated with parenting are deeply ingrained. Whether it's checking your homework or participating in decision-making, their involvement in various aspects of your life has become second nature. Shifting toward a less controlling relationship can indeed be challenging.
- **Shifting Expectations:** Sometimes, expectations parents have regarding your college experience may not align with your reality or desires. Whether it's the desire for you to follow in their footsteps, share their values and goals, or chart a specific path, they may grapple with reconciling their aspirations with your unique journey.

Growing Up and Moving On

Responsibility is a badge of honor that we should proudly wear, not something to lament. It may not always be visible, but it shines through our actions in various ways. One of its first gleams is found in keeping promises. When you make a commitment, it's essential to follow through. This consistency allows people to place their trust in you, akin to a steadfast bridge enduring even the fiercest storms.

Time management is another facet of responsibility. Respecting your own time, as well as others', is significant. Being punctual for meetings, dates, or events conveys a message of respect and seriousness, saying, "I value you, and I take our engagements seriously."

Financial responsibility is yet another indicator of maturity. It's not about having vast wealth; it's about using your resources wisely. In today's uncertain world, financial stability can provide a sense of security and hope. When you make a mistake, taking responsibility and owning up to it is essential. Blaming others may be the easy way out, but acknowledging your errors requires courage and maturity. Being proactive is also a demonstration of responsibility. It means not waiting passively but taking the lead, investing effort, and actively participating in tasks and endeavors.

The Unbroken Threads

Let's talk about Jane and her dad, Tom. Growing up, Jane was her father Tom's most cherished treasure. As she prepared to embark on her journey into college life, leaving behind her small-town roots, Tom was filled with pride, but beneath that, a nagging fear loomed. It wasn't just the typical separation anxiety; it was the fear of an uncertain future he couldn't control or shield her from.

During her initial weeks at college, Jane found herself in a whirlwind of new faces, friendships, and newfound freedoms. Tom's calls were met with quick reassurances like, "I'm good, Dad. Gotta run!" But these rushed responses left Tom feeling uneasy. He was worried about his daughter's well-being and couldn't help but wonder what she was up to, who she was spending time with, and if she was safe.

For Jane, college was a chance to express her individuality, and she saw her father's concerns as nothing more than restrictions. She felt like he was questioning her integrity, which led to arguments and misunderstandings. Tom's wife, Maria, saw the growing divide between them and empathized with Tom's anxiety while understanding Jane's desire for independence. Despite their efforts to bridge the gap, Jane's resistance only grew stronger. Over time, their once-strong connection dwindled, replaced by anger and silence.

As Jane stopped confiding in her parents, her academic performance suffered, and she made misguided decisions, all in the name of autonomy. When summer finally arrived, Jane returned home a shadow of her former self. During a family dinner, emotions overflowed. Jane's composed exterior crumbled, revealing her insecurities and need for guidance. Tom, equally moved, shared his fears and his desire to protect her, realizing that he needed to let go of control.

Their heartfelt exchange marked a new beginning. Together, they worked to rebuild their bond, a slow process filled with understanding and acceptance of each other's imperfections. By the time Jane's second year of college began, they had found a balance between independence and guidance. Tom recognized Jane's maturity, and Jane understood that growing older didn't mean growing apart. Their college years became a time of growth not only for Jane but also for Tom. They both learned that faith, communication, and empathy were crucial in preserving their connection. They had to evolve, mature, and transform to find their way back to each other.

Through it all, they realized that the love between a parent and child could endure, adapt, and flourish, even in the face of fears, misunderstandings, and immaturity. This understanding became a symbol of their unbreakable bond.

Maintaining a Supportive and Connected Relationship

As the holiday season approaches, college students, now seasoned with newfound independence, prepare to return home. It's a time to embrace the familial warmth, relish in the nostalgia of home-cooked meals, and find solace in the familiarity of one's surroundings. Yet, this homecoming is also a delicate balancing act, a dance between the autonomy cultivated during campus life and the shared expectations of being back home. In this intricate tango, two key components come into play: setting boundaries and distributing household responsibilities. Let's delve into the heart of these matters.

Ground Rules: Building the Pillars of Mutual Respect

The academic world grants students the freedom to foster personal growth and independence. It's a time when you learn to live life on your terms, and sometimes, these newfound ways of living don't seamlessly align with your family's home environment. Unsurprisingly, returning home can lead to some friction, akin to a cultural shock.

To preempt potential conflicts, it's crucial to initiate clear communication regarding expectations and boundaries right from the start. This dialogue should be an opportunity to respect and consider both your perspectives and your parents'. Topics may encompass curfews, visitors, personal space, and even culinary preferences.

It's equally important to encourage a two-way understanding. While your parents may have concerns about certain aspects of your behavior, you also have the right to express your evolved lifestyle and thought processes. The aim is to reach a mutual understanding and, when necessary, find a middle ground that respects your identity as a college student while honoring your family's values.

Domestic Duties

Transitioning from the relatively relaxed atmosphere of college life to the more structured home environment often raises questions about household responsibilities. Who is responsible for what? Are college students expected to participate in household chores, and if so, to what extent?

To set clear expectations, open dialogue once again plays a crucial role. It's essential for you and your parents to have discussions about the division of household tasks, including cooking, cleaning, and taking care of younger siblings or pets.

Finding the right balance is key. While it's reasonable to expect your contribution to household chores, recognizing your unique circumstances may require some flexibility. For instance, if you're returning home to study or work part-time, adjusting the chore schedule could be beneficial.

Engaging in household tasks should not be seen as an imposition. Instead, consider it an opportunity to make a positive contribution to the family and strengthen your bonds. It allows your parents to witness your growth, and in turn, you can contribute to enhancing the family dynamic.

Additional Items When Navigating Transitions Between College and Home:

Shifting between college life and returning home during breaks can be a bit of a rollercoaster. You might experience what's called "reverse culture shock" as you adapt to being back in your hometown. To help smooth out this adjustment:

Keep the Lines of Communication Open:

Staying connected with your family is key. Share your college experiences and the changes you've gone through while listening to their stories too. It can make the transition back home much smoother.

Coping with Change:

Change is a constant in life, and moving towards adulthood and independence can be a real challenge, both for you and your parents. Here's how to navigate this period of change:

Patience and Understanding:

Be patient with yourself and your family as everyone adapts to new roles and dynamics. Understand that change can be uncertain, but it's also an opportunity for growth and development.

Taking Care of Your Mental Health:

Your mental health is super important during this time. College can bring on stress and anxiety, so here's what you should know:

Seek Support: Don't hesitate to reach out for support when needed. Your college probably offers mental health resources, and there are local services at home too. Never forget to prioritize your mental well-being.

Being Money-Savvy:

Let's talk finances! Managing your money is a crucial part of growing up. Here's what you need to know:

Budgeting: Learn the ropes of budgeting. Create a monthly budget to keep track of your income and expenses. It's a great way to manage your finances responsibly.

Open Talks About Money: Have honest conversations with your parents about financial matters. Discuss your financial responsibilities and how you can help with expenses at home. It's all about being open and transparent.

Resolving Conflicts:

Conflicts can happen; it's a part of life. Here's how to deal with them effectively:

Effective Communication: Practice good communication skills. Listen actively, express your thoughts and feelings respectfully, and aim to understand each other's perspectives. Finding common ground can help resolve disagreements.

Setting Your Goals:

Setting goals, both personal and academic, is a fantastic habit. Here's why:

Personal Growth: Goal-setting is all about personal growth and success. During college breaks, set clear goals for yourself to stay motivated and focused. These goals can cover everything from your studies to your personal development.

Seeking Guidance:

Don't hesitate to reach out for help and guidance during your college years:

Connect with Mentors: Professors, advisors, and counselors are here to support you. Reach out to them for advice as you navigate your academic and personal journey. Building these relationships can be incredibly helpful.

The Role of Siblings:

If you have siblings, they're a part of your family dynamic too:

Understanding Siblings: Your siblings might also be adjusting to your presence at home. Try to understand their perspective and feelings during this transition. Open and empathetic communication can strengthen your relationship with them.

Building Resilience:

Challenges and change can make you stronger:

Embrace Challenges: Face challenges as opportunities for growth. Overcoming obstacles during your college years will build resilience and prepare you for the future. Remember, you're more capable than you might think.

The Power of Self-Reflection:

Self-reflection is a super useful tool:

Self-Assessment: Engage in self-reflection activities like journaling or self-assessment exercises. These practices can help you gain insights into your personal growth and development. It's a great way to make the most of your college experience and transitions.

These tips and insights are here to help you navigate the exciting but sometimes tricky journey of college life and beyond. If you ever need more guidance or have specific questions, feel free to ask. Your journey is worth savoring and making the most of!

Key Takeaways

- Stepping over the threshold from youth into adulthood, you face a kaleidoscope of challenges and treasures. Think of it as a mystery box— brimming with lessons in life skills such as whipping up a meal, budgeting wisely, and ensuring your home doesn't crumble into disarray. You're also met with fresh responsibilities, such as starting your first job or immersing yourself in the buzz of university life.
- Drawing from the narrative of Jane and her father, Tom, the text spotlights the pivotal role communication and understanding play in parent-child relationships. Misinterpretations and roadblocks in communication can create fissures, affecting trust, academic prowess, and mental wellness. Open dialogue and a healthy dose of empathy form the cornerstone of healing and growth.

AFTERWORD

As we reach the conclusion of this book, it becomes abundantly clear that college is not merely a stepping stone to the "real world." It's a vibrant and transformative world of its own, filled with a myriad of opportunities, friendships, triumphs, failures, laughter, and tears. Above all, it's a realm of immense personal growth.

Picture this: You are now standing at the threshold of an exciting new chapter where classrooms transcend mere textbooks and lectures. They become arenas of debate, innovation, and discovery. Your professors are not just instructors; they can be your mentors, guiding you on your quest for knowledge. While navigating the academic landscape is a significant part of your college journey, it's only one piece of the puzzle.

Throughout your college experience, you'll discover joy in extracurricular activities, resilience during late-night cramming sessions, and tenacity in coffee-fueled morning classes. Undoubtedly, you'll face challenges, from financial constraints to overwhelming stress. These challenges, however, are not mere obstacles; they are catalysts that will shape you into a stronger, more compassionate individual.

But here's the secret to thriving in college – you are never alone on this adventure. Reach out for help when needed, whether it's leaning on your friends, seeking guidance from professors, or utilizing counseling services. Your college community is there to support you through every trial and triumph.

In addition to overcoming challenges, don't forget to have fun. Explore new hobbies, attend campus events, join clubs and societies, and dance like no one's watching at college festivals. College is a time of self-discovery, and embracing every facet of it, from academics to extracurriculars, is key to your personal growth.

So, as we raise a toast to your college years, remember this: Be bold, be inquisitive, and, above all, be yourself. Approach college with an open heart, a curious mind, and an eagerness to grow. This is your story to write, so make it a masterpiece! Your college journey is an incredible adventure, and you have all the tools you need to make it a truly remarkable chapter in your life. Cheers to the exciting journey ahead!

BIBLIOGRAPHY

- Arnold Schwarzenegger Quotes. (n.d.). BrainyQuote. https://www.brainyquote.com/quotes/arnold_schwarzenegger_116694

- Boogaard, K. (2021, December 26). How to write SMART goals. https://www.atlassian.com/blog/productivity/how-to-write-smart-goals#:~:text=What%20are%20SMART%20-goals%3F,within%20a%20certain%

- 20time%20frame.

- Duncan, A. (2013, April 23). Education: The most powerful weapon for changing the world. USAID. https://blog.usaid.-gov/2013/04/education-the-most-powerful-weapon/

- Misty Copeland quotes. (n.d.). BrainyQuote. https://www.brainyquote.com/quotes/misty_copeland_749724 More than 50% of gen z college students report feeling lonely according to sodexo student lifestyle survey. (2022, August 9). Sodexo. https://us.sodexo.com/media/news-releases/gen-z-college-students-lonely.html

- Rainer Maria Rilke quotes. (n.d.). BrainyQuote. https://www.brainyquote.com/quotes/rainer_maria_rilke_147758

- Richard Bach quotes. (n.d.). BrainyQuote. https://www.brainyquote.com/quotes/richard_bach_134891

- Socrates quotes. (n.d.). BrainyQuote. https://www.brainyquote.com/quotes/socrates_101212

- The reflection of education that you can use to change the world. (n.d.). 123HelpMe.https://www.123helpme.com/essay/The-Reflection-Of-Education-That-You-

CanFC6A69UD26#:~:text=%E2%80%9CEduca-tion%20is%20the%20most%20powerful, (Martin%20Luther%20King%20Jr).

- 31 alarming college student mental health statistics. (2022, August 2). What to Become. https://whattobecome.com/blog/college-student-mental-health-statistics/
- Thomas Merton quotes. (n.d.). BrainyQuote. https://www.brainyquote.com/quotes/thomas_merton_385072

Made in the USA
Las Vegas, NV
27 June 2024

91554125R00090